The Little Church in the Wildwood

Preachers and Fried Chicken

Terry Keeling
P.O. Box 7
Leona, TX 75850
903-536-7708

Terry Keeling

SUNBELT EAKIN   Austin, Texas

FIRST EDITION
Copyright © 2005
By Terry Keeling
Published in the U.S.A.
By Sunbelt Eakin Press
A Division of Sunbelt Media, Inc.
P.O. Drawer 90159
Austin, Texas 78709-0159
email: sales@eakinpress.com
website: www.eakinpress.com
ALL RIGHTS RESERVED.
1   2   3   4   5   6   7   8   9
ISBN 978-1-57168-087-7
ISBN 1-57168-087-X
Library of Congress Control Number 2005936669

Contents

iii

v

Preface

In more than thirty-five years of traveling down lots of country roads, selling farms and ranches, I have seen lots of little country churches – and I have noticed that a lot of them are disappearing.

Several years ago, I started taking pictures of some of the more interesting looking of these old churches . . . and, at the same time I began to become interested in the history of some of them. Having grown up in a small country church myself, I have always been very much aware of how important these old churches have always been to the folks who grew up in them.

It was not long after . . . sometime in 2001, that I decided to put some this information—and photos—down in book form. The result is what follows.

I did not attempt to cover the entire state—or even an entire portion of the state. Such a project would be beyond the scope of a single book. I covered basically the counties of Ft. Bend, Wharton, Lavaca, Waller, Grimes, Madison, Leon and Houston . . . an area in which I travel regularly. I was not even able to cover all the churches in these counties. I concentrated on country churches . . . with the exception of one or two "gray area" churches, I did not cover any churches in town. I also concentrated on the churches that look like "old country churches." I stayed away from those that had nice, modern looking brick buildings.

It is my contention that country churches are not built of simply boards and nails . . . they are made of flesh and blood—people—as well. I have tried to capture that human aspect. I have tried to present not just the pure history of the churches, but something of the human interest aspect as well . . . the people to whom that church is and has been so important.

My only regret is that I could not include every church I came across. There were some that we simply couldn't come up with the necessary information on . . . in many cases, the church had burned at some point, and with it the church records had been lost.

The limitations of space have precluded the inclusion of more than the number of churches included herein. Perhaps, in a subsequent book, we can do more.

Acknowledgments

This project could not possibly have been completed without the help and assistance of a large number of wonderful people.

Thanks to Bailey Teter for doing the illustrations used herein.

Thanks to the folks at Cameras Unlimited, in Rosenberg, for their expert help in handling all of my photo processing needs . . . even when I occasionally had some unusual—and difficult—requests/needs.

Thanks to Ms. Eliza Bishop, at the Houston County Historical Commission, in Crockett, for her invaluable help in supplying needed information and in putting me in contact with other individuals who were able to provide me with needed information.

Thanks to Mrs. Faye Boutotte, at the Leon County Historical Commission, in Centerville, for helping me with information on Leon County churches.

Thanks to Charles Young, Ashford and Oliver Funeral Home, in Navasota, for helping to put me in contact with individuals in Grimes County who were able to help me with needed information. Ditto to Leroy Singleton, Singleton Funeral Home, Hempstead, for giving me similar assistance in Grimes and Waller Counties.

Thanks to Jane Miller, Grimes County Chamber of Commerce, in Navasota, for helping me out with information on Grimes County churches.

And—last but far from least—thanks to all those individuals who were willing and able to help me with information about a particular church or churches—along with their own personal feelings and recollections.

"Thanks, Guys . . . I couldn't have done it without you!!!"

The Church in the Wildwood

There's a church in the valley by the wildwood
No lovelier spot in the dale
No place is so dear to my child-hood
As the little brown church in the vale

Oh, come to the church in the wildwood
to the trees where the wild flowers bloom
Where the parting hymn will be chanted
We will weep by the side of the tomb

How sweet on a clear Sabbath morning
To list to the clear ringing bell
Its tones so sweetly are calling
Oh, come to the church in the vale

Pleasant Hill Baptist Chruch, Ft. Bend County

1

From the church in the valley by the wildwood
When day fades away into night
I would fain from this spot of my child-hood
Wing my way to the mansions of light

CHORUS:
Come to the church in the wildwood
Oh come to the church in the vale
No spot is so dear to my child-hood
as the little brown church in the vale"

When Dr. William Pitts wrote this old, old hymn, so many years ago, he probably had one particular church in mind. However, in my travels over the years, I've seen a lot of "little churches in the wildwood". Each one has its own individual personality—its own identity—its own history—but they all share one common characteristic. To the people who attend that church—and the people who grew up in that church—that particular church truly is "that little brown church in the vale".

My own "Church in the Wildwood" is the Evans Chapel Methodist Church in Leon County (East Texas). I was baptized in that church ... I grew up in that church. Both my parents ... all four of my grandparents ... five of my great-grandparents ... and one of my great-great-grandparents are buried in the cemetery there behind the church. Some day (I hope it's not soon) I will probably be buried there ...

"Where the parting hymn will be chanted, we will weep by the side of the tomb."

I think it is probably safe to say that the folks who grew up in the Shiloh Primitive Baptist Church ... or the Two-Mile Methodist Church ... or the Clear Creek Baptist Church ... or the Mt. Olive Baptist Church ... or any other similar small country church ... feel the same way about their particular church ...

"No spot is so dear to my child-hood as the little brown church in the vale."

In my thirty-plus years as a real estate broker, selling farms and ranches, I've traveled down lots of country roads throughout the eastern half of Texas. In the process, I've seen many, many country churches. Each one is different . . . each one has a story to tell . . . but the overall pattern is pretty much the same.

East Texas—the area east of the Brazos River—was pretty much settled by folks who came there from the "Old South" (Alabama, Mississippi, Georgia, Tennessee, etc.). This is true, for the most part, of both the White and the Black populations. Between the Brazos and the Colorado rivers can be found a mixture of both the Old South culture and the German-Czech culture, but in East Texas, it was almost exclusively the Old South culture. These Old South settlers brought with them their culture, their heritage, their traditions . . . and their religion. Religion was a very, very important part of their lives—for both the Whites and the Blacks. Most were Methodist or Baptist. In the towns and cities could be found other denominations, but out in the rural areas it was almost entirely Methodist or Baptist. I'm not sure why, but that's the way it was.

There are some cynics who have suggested that these folks were all Methodist or Baptist because they couldn't spell Episicopaleon or Presibeterian . . . but I don't believe that for a minute. I personally know several Methodists—and two or three Baptists—who can both spell and pronounce Epsci . . . Espic . . . Ecip . . . Perib . . . Praab . . . Presib . . . those other two denominations. (Actually, during those early years, the Methodist and Episcopal churches were one—they didn't split apart until later.)

Music was very important to these early settlers . . . it was a vital

Macedonia Baptist Church, Grimes County

part of their religion . . . both for the Blacks and the Whites. There was nothing subtle or timid about their music. It tended to be strong, loud and forceful . . . songs that have lived on even until today . . . songs like "Marching to Zion," "Rock of Ages," "Swing Low, Sweet Chariot," "Bringing in the Sheaves," "Down by the Riverside," "Go Down, Moses," "Amazing Grace," "Sweet Bye and Bye," and others of a similar nature. Everyone was expected to join in the singing, regardless of the quality of that person's voice. Often, there would be all-day music programs (we called them Singing Conventions) at the church.

Most of these areas were first settled in the mid to late 1800s, with a very heavy migration immediately after the end of the Civil War. In most cases, as soon as they had enough people in a given community, they formed a church. Most of the White churches were formed between 1850 and 1900. Most of the Black churches, however, were formed within a twenty-year "window"—between 1870 and 1890—the period immediately after Emancipation. Contrary to what many people might believe, most slaves had a re-ligious background. There were many traveling preachers (both Black and White) who periodically visited the farms and plantations and preached to the slaves. In many, many cases, the slaves attended church, on a regular basis, with their owners. After Emancipation, the freed Blacks still had their religious background—but they had no churches. After a period of adjustment to their new circum-stances, they began to remedy that deficiency . . . they began to build churches.

In those early times—and continuing almost to the present time, churches in the rural areas (more so than churches in the towns) played a vital role in the social—as well as the spiritual—lives of the members. Along with the school, the church was the focal point of the community. This was particularly true in the "old days" when we were a less mobile society. In addition to the usual Sunday church services, there would be regular activities—some of a religious nature and some that were purely social—at the church throughout the week. In my childhood, I can remember ice cream socials, group "Cemetery Workings," Singing Conventions, and others. In those rural communities, there were very, very few resi-dents who were not active in the church. In influencing and shap-ing the lives of those who grew up in these rural communities, the churches were probably second in importance only to the parents—and it would probably be a very close second.

These tended to be very stable churches, with very stable memberships. They were churches where a tiny baby might be baptized . . . and, then, seventy or eighty or ninety years later, that same person would be "funeralized" and "sent on home" in that same church. They were churches where extended generations of the same family sat in the same pew(s) every Sunday for many years . . . that was their pew, and no one else was allowed to sit there.

During and after World War II, we saw the migration from the farms to the cities—and the rural churches began to see their membership rolls drop—a trend that has continued almost to the present. In recent years, however, the population in many rural communities has somewhat stabilized. Many of the young people still leave to go to the city to "seek their fortune," but this is offset by the folks that come back when they retire. It's sort of a "wash." For the Black population, however, this has, in many cases, not been true. The Black population in most of these rural communities is rapidly and steadily declining . . . and aging. It is estimated that the average age of Blacks in these rural communities (and within the Black churches) is probably over sixty—and is increasing. Many of the Black churches, faced with a drastically declining membership, are struggling to survive—some have already closed—others have adjusted to a "part-time schedule" with services on something less than an every Sunday basis. Sadly, it is likely that many of these churches will close and disappear over the next ten to twenty years.

Mt. Airie–Keechi Baptist Church, Leon County

In many cases, there simply will not be enough members left to enable them to survive.

While some of these churches undoubtedly will physically close and cease to exist in the next few years, they will live on through the people who grew up there—who were influenced forever by what they learned and were taught there.

From the church in the valley by the wildwood
when day fades away into night
I would fain from this spot of my child-hood
Wing my way to the mansions of light

Come to the church in the wildwood
Oh, come to the church in the vale;
No spot is so dear to my child-hood
as the little brown church in the vale

Independence Baptist Church, Grimes County (inactive)

Preachers and Fried Chicken

"He was afraid to take that last piece of chicken."

"Terry, I need you to go out in the back yard and get me a couple of fryers. This is our Sunday to bring the preacher home for dinner, and I need to get as much of it ready as I can before we go to church."

Mother was calling out her instructions from the kitchen. It was early Sunday morning, sometime in the mid-1940s, and we were preparing to go to church, as we did every Sunday morning, at the Evans Chapel Methodist Church, in the community where I grew up, near Leona, in East Texas (Leon County).

At that time, and even into the 1950s, it was customary in most country churches for someone in the congregation to take the preacher and his family home for dinner, after church was over. (Note: I'm referring to the noon meal—the word "lunch" wasn't in our vocabulary at that time.) The preachers didn't get paid very much . . . and this was one of the 'perks' of the job. We never referred to them as "ministers"—they were "preachers."

The preachers knew this . . . they expected it . . . and some say they prepared for it. There was speculation that some of these preachers might fast all day Saturday in preparation for the free meal coming up on Sunday. I don't know if this was true or not . . . but I can remember seeing some preachers put away an unbelievable amount of food at our table.

When it was our turn to bring the preacher home for dinner, Mother would fix most of the meal early that morning before we went to church. She would have her peas cooked, the potato salad ready, the pecan pie cooked, the corn bread mixed up and ready, and the chicken cut up and ready to fry. When we got back to the house after church, all she had to do was warm up the peas, put the corn-

7

bread in the oven, and fry the chicken. It seems it was almost always fried chicken that we had for Sunday dinner. Maybe that was because we always had chickens available.

The abundance of chicken may be what led to the almost legendary affinity Methodist preachers (I think the same was true of Baptist preachers, as well) had for fried chicken. I am told that with regard to the world's record for the most fried chicken consumed at one sitting, the first 100 spots on the list are held by Methodist and/or Baptist preachers. I haven't been able to confirm this, but based on my childhood observations, I don't doubt it for a minute.

As Mother had instructed me, I went out in the back yard and chased down two fryers. It took me a while—they were pretty fast—but I finally caught two of them and wrung their necks. I picked them, cleaned them, washed them off, and took them inside to Mother. She cut them up, washed them again, and put them in the refrigerator. She had already cooked the peas and fixed the potato salad.

Mother gave my brother, Royce, and me our final instructions on how we were to behave while the preacher was here. He was to get first choice on all the food—we would have to take whatever was left. As soon as she finished all her preparations, we went on to church.

Our preacher at that time (I'll call him Brother Smith) was a tall, lanky man who always looked hungry. He and Sister Smith followed us home as soon as church was over. We all sat down on the front porch and waited while Mother finished up the meal. It didn't take her very long. As soon as it was ready, we all sat down at the table, and Mother brought in the platter of fried chicken and set it down right in front of Brother Smith . . . she knew that's where it would wind up anyway. Mother asked Brother Smith to say the blessing. Normally, he was pretty long winded when he preached . . . but with that platter of fried chicken right in front of his face, he cut it pretty short.

Once Brother Smith started in to eating, he didn't talk very much. He was an ambidextrous eater . . . he could handle a drumstick in either hand. Once in a while, you could even see him with a drumstick in each hand, at the same time.

After about twenty minutes, Brother Smith had to loosen his belt a couple of notches. This was about the same time that Mother brought in the second platter of chicken. Finally, we wound up with one piece of chicken left on the platter. Brother Smith had manners . . . either that, or it was that stern warning look that Sister Smith gave him. At any rate, he wouldn't take it. He looked at it . . . a lot. You could even see little beads of sweat breaking out on his forehead . . . and he got a little bit of a twitch at the corner of his mouth . . . but he wouldn't take it. However, he had more than his share of the peas, potato salad and cornbread . . . but he wouldn't take that last piece of chicken. You could tell it took a whole a lot of self-control for him to leave it there on the platter.

Besides, I guess he had to save room for the pecan pie. After about forty minutes, most of the food was gone, and we all got up from the table, went outside, and sat down on the front porch, to let the food settle for awhile. Brother Smith still didn't talk very much—but he looked pretty contented.

Things have changed, as they always do. Nobody takes the preacher home for dinner any more. I've often wondered if preachers are still addicted to fried chicken. Maybe that's something they learned at divinity school . . . I don't know.

Sometimes, I miss that Sunday dinner with the preacher.

Shiloh Primitive Baptist Church

HOUSTON COUNTY

"He was guilty of 'disorderly walking' . . . and they kicked him out of the church."

The Shiloh Primitive Baptist Church is unique among old country churches in that since its very first organizational meeting, the church has held regular monthly meetings, or conferences, and detailed minutes were written each time—and those minutes are still available (unlike many country churches, this church never burned). Consequently, we have a much more complete record of the Shiloh Church's early history than is normally the case.

Located three miles east of Grapeland, on FM 227, the church

Shiloh Primitive Baptist Church

10

was formally organized on April 7, 1866. According to the minutes, the founding members were Samuel Matthews, William Lagore, J. A. Smith, Lavisa Matthews, Lucy Smith, J.F.M. Cunningham, Eliza J. Cunningham, Mary Ann Denson, E. A. Garrett, Hannah Stowe, Eliza Brooks, John D. Matthews, S. A. Matthews, Joel Stowe, H. H. Whitehead, Mary Ann Whitehead, B. M. Clewis, J. C. Green, C. Blanchard, H. L. Matthews, Prudence Lane, J. D. Bynum, and Mary Bynum.

Strict rules of procedure and conduct were established for their monthly conferences—among them the following—"No person shall speak more than three times to the same subject without leave of the moderator or church"—"There shall be no whispering, talking, laughing or walking idly about during the time of the conference"—"Nor no male member shall excuse himself from the conference while in session without leave"—"Any male member absenting himself from the conference three times in succession, they shall be sent after by the church unless the cause be known."

According to Houston County Deed Records, on Nov. 20, 1884, S. M. and Levia Matthews gave 1.5 acres of land to the church "for the purpose of building a house for a place of worship . . . to have and to hold for . . . as long as the said Shiloh Church exists and holds to the old Primitive Baptist Doctrine faith and order or as long as said land is used for a place of worship for the old Baptist faith and order . . . ."

The first pastor was Rev. Benjamin Parker. He was one of the many Parker family members that came to Texas from Illinois in the early 1830s. Some of the Parker families moved on to Limestone County and established the ill-fated Fort Parker. Several of them were killed in the infamous Indian raid in 1836 (when Cynthia Ann Parker was captured). Most of the survivors returned to Anderson County and/or Houston County.

With the exception of a two year interruption (1867 and 1868), Rev. Parker served as pastor until 1895.

Over the years, the Shiloh Church has expected its members to adhere to very strict standards of behavior and has not hesitated to "call on the carpet" those members who failed to adhere to those standards. The minutes reflect a number of instances in which members were disciplined (Author's note—to spare any embarrassment to present descendants of those members who were disciplined, we have changed their real names to the "generic" names of Smith or Jones).

April 1874—"First the church preferred charges against Brother Jones for using bad language, and walking disorderly, and absenting himself from the church" (The following month, Brother Jones was "excluded from the membership of the church").

July 1874—"received Sister Smith, who had been dismissed by letter from this church and had joined the missionaries, but now makes confession that she done wrong and returns."

September 1874—"Brother Smith acknowledges he has done wrong by joining the temperance society and says he will not visit the society no more."

April 1875—"First the church preferred charges against Brother Jones for living in adultery, and drinking spirits or whiskey to excess and swearing, and he was excluded from the fellowship of the church."

June 1888—"Preferred a charge against Sister Smith for absenting herself from the church and joining the Farmers Alliance, a secret institution. The church withdrew fellowship with Sister Smith for the above charges."

August 1888—"Appointed a committee to visit Brother Jones and ascertain the reason of his absence from conference."

August 1890—"Preferred a charge against Brother Smith for getting drunk and visiting the race track. Appointed a committee to notify Brother Smith of the charge against him and to be at the next conference."

August 1890—"Taken up reference and withdrew fellowship with Brother Smith."

November 1891—"Preferred a charge against Brother Jones for living in adultery. Appointed a committee to notify him of the charge . . . and to cite him to conference."

January 1892—"the church withdrew fellowship with Brother Jones."

August 1896—"The church preferred a charge against Brother Smith for withdrawing from Communion and partaking of, what they call the Lords Supper, with another church . . . not of our faith and order, and appointed a committee . . . to notify him of the charge."

September 1896—"The church withdrew fellowship with Brother Smith."

February 1898—"Preferred a charge against Brother Jones for attending parties and for participating in them and refusing to make reconciliation to the church."

January 1899—"Preferred a charge against Brother Smith for going to parties and dancing, also preferred a charge against Brother Jones for visiting the ballroom and dancing and participating in gambling and raffling off a watch. Appointed a committee to notify the brethren of the charge."

June 1905—"Preferred a charge against Sister Smith for leaving Brother Smith and living with him."

June 1917—Brother Jones made acknowledgement for marrying a divorced person which was received."

June, 1938—"Received a letter from Salem Church charging that we were fellowshipping adultery in Shiloh Church. The letter was read . . . and tabled . . . and ignored." July, 1946—"After which the church went into communion, and took the bread and wine and also washed each others feet. After which we sang a hymn and went out."

The Shiloh Primitive Baptist Church has functioned continuously since its formation. "I'm ninety-two years old" says Mrs.

Mrs. Ethel Clark

Ethyl (Weisinger) Clark, "And I've been a part of the Shiloh church since I was a baby. The church was like family to me. My mother died when I was six years old—and until my daddy later remarried, the folks in the church helped raise me. My daddy, Paul Edward Weisinger, was ordained as a minister in this church, in 1925. He pastored the church for forty-four years, from 1928 till he died in 1972.

"When I was a teenager, the church was always full," says Mrs. Clark, "but so many have moved away or died. We're down now to just two members—myself and my sister-in-law. We have church once a month—our pastor is Rev. Wade Johnson—and we usually have ten or twelve folks there. I don't know how much longer we can hold on. It's sad. This church has so many memories. I like to visit other churches . . . but the Shiloh Church is my church . . . It always will be."

Rev. Paul Edward Weisinger
—Courtesy of Mrs. Clark

Robinson Hill Baptist Church,

GRIMES COUNTY

"They hooked mules to the building and turned it around."

"I joined the Robinson Hill Baptist Church in 1943, when I was eleven years old," recounts Jack Bowen. "As far as I know, there's not any written history of the church, but I know a little bit about it—just from what I remember hearing from some of the older folks."

It is believed the church was formed in 1894. Deed Records show that in that year, a Mr. and Mrs. Bates donated five acres of land for a church.

"I was always told the Robinson Hill Church was a "split-off" from the Longstreet Baptist Church over in Montgomery County. Some of the early families were Bates, Dean, Bowen, and Williams.

Robinson Hill Baptist Church

15

My grandfather, Rev. Jim Bowen, served as pastor of the church for awhile, but I don't know when. I remember hearing about a Rev. Jones, Rev. S. W. Davis, Rev. King, Rev. Murphy, and Rev. D. W. Mitchell—but I don't know when any of them served."

It is believed the original church building burned—but it is not known when—and was replaced by the building that is still there today.

According to Mr. Bowen, "This building was turned around to face a different direction. They changed the course of the road and the members decided to turn the church around to face towards the new road—so they put logs underneath the building, hooked mules to it and turned it to the way they wanted it to face."

Located on FM 2819, south of Richards, the Robinson Hill Church is still there, though the membership is small. The faithful few still have preaching once a month and Sunday School every Sunday. As Mr. Bowen says, "This church has been a big, big part of our lives for a long, long time, and we hope it continues that way for a long time still to come."

Tanyard Methodist Church

MADISON COUNTY

"We're still faithful . . . and we will be till we're called home."

The Tanyard Methodist Church is located on FM 1119, northeast of Madisonville, in the Tanyard Community. The community got its name from a tannery, or tanning yard that functioned there, in the 1800s, tanning cowhides.

Mrs. Edgar Mae (Nealey) Sueing is a daughter-in-law of one of the founding members of the Tanyard Church, Mack Sueing. She and her daughter, Linda Sueing Jackson, have done extensive research on the history of the church. They believe the church was established in September 1896, and was first located on the M. C. Sueing place. The founding trustees were Mack Sueing, Dan Nealey and J. L. Proctor. It is believed the church was moved to its present location in 1922—that building is the one still in use today.

Tanyard Methodist Church.

17

Mrs. Edgar Mae Sueing

Some of the early pastors were the Reverends Scripture, Pace, Blue, Mays, Shaw, Taylor, Crockett, Sneed, Sams, Polk, Lamb and Williams. Early church leaders, in addition to the founding trustees, included Edgar Nealey, Lacey Washington and Dick Washington.

"I joined the church as a small child. I'm seventy-seven now, and I can't remember ever not being a member" recounts Mrs. Sueing. "My daddy, Edgar Nealey, died two or three months before I was born . . . and until my mother later remarried, the folks in that church, along with my older brother, sort of helped raise me. I'm not the oldest member . . . Mrs. Rhodie Mae Johnson is ninety . . . but I've probably been a member longer than anybody else.

"In the old days, the church was also the social center of the community. We always had big crowds at church back then. Most folks came in wagons . . . some rode horseback . . . there were a few buggies . . . and some walked . . . but they all came—almost every Sunday.

"The church was like family to us back then. We knew everybody there—most of us were kin—and we all helped one another out whenever help was needed.

"Our crowds are small now" Mrs. Sueing laments. "We don't have many young folks anymore . . . they have all moved away. We still have church one Sunday a month . . . Rev. Carey Cauley, Jr. is our pastor.

"Even though we're few in numbers, we're still faithful . . . and we will be till we're called home."

Dickson Hopewell Baptist Church

HOUSTON COUNTY

We carried our good shoes in our hands.

Unlike many of the small country churches, there are fairly complete records of the history of the Dickson Hopewell Baptist Church, from its beginning, in 1870, right up to the present. According to Mrs. Barbara Murphy, a life-long member of the church, "I got all this information from my mother, Mrs. Willie M. Smith and from Mrs. Georgia Jolley, before they died—and I wrote it down."

According to Mrs. Murphy's information, several families of freed slaves settled in what is now the Dickson Hopewell Community, west of Crockett, in 1865. Among these early families were Dickson, Harrison, Jolley, Fobbs, Jenkins, Scott, Smith, and Woods.

Along about 1870, they decided they needed a church. Winston and Lizzie Dickson gave land for a site and the members built a

Dickson-Hopewell Church

19

church—a large building with a steeple on each side and a large bell in the middle. They named it the Dickson Hopewell Baptist Church.

The charter members were Winston and Lizzie Dickson, Toby and Martha Smith, Syou Cooper and his wife, Saul and Ellen Woods, Nelson and Ellen Bailey, Sterling and Moriah Fobbs, Willie and Tillie Baines, Charles and Abbey Jenkins, Joe and Fannie Jolley, Joshua and Harriett Smith, Mango and Elosia Delane, Henry and Sina Campbell, Henry and Emma Baines, and Mrs. Mary Jolley. Descendents of these original members still live in the community today and many of them are active in the church.

The first pastor was Rev. Pap Robertson and the first deacons were Nelson Bailey, Syou Cooper, Lewis Gill, Isaac Smith, Lewis Ewing, and Jimmy Johnson.

The second pastor was Rev. Robert Groves. It was under his leadership that a school was established near the church. Later pastors included Rev. I. P. Hunt, Rev. W. B. Scott, Rev. J. H. Simpson, and Rev. J. T. Groves (son of Rev. Robert Groves).

Mrs. Robin Roberts recalls growing up in the Dickson Hopewell Church (Her mother was a Fobbs) and attending the church as a child. "We had to walk to church" she recalls "and when it rained, that red mud got real bad on those roads we had to walk along . . . so, we would wear our old shoes and carry our good shoes in our hands. When we got to the church, we would take off our old, muddy shoes and leave them outside. We would put on our good shoes and wear them till we got ready to leave. Then we would put our old shoes back on and walk back home . . . again holding our good shoes in our hands."

Over the years, the Dickson Hopewell Baptist Church has sent thirteen of its sons into the ministry: Rev. Henry Baines, Rev. West Smith, Rev. Harrison Fobbs, Rev. Emmett Dickson, Rev. Melvin Dickson, Rev. Albert Smith, Rev. Mango Delane, Rev. Joe Jolley, Rev. A. R. Smith, Rev. Joe Smith, Rev. Clevester Smith, Rev. Robert Jolley, and Rev. Harry Fred Smith.

Rev. Jay Lee is the present pastor of the church. Under his leadership, the church still conducts regular services and continues to serve its members—and the community. As Mrs. Murphy puts it, "The Dickson Hopewell Baptist Church has been so important to the people of this community through all these years . . . and it still is."

Clear Creek Baptist Church

LEON COUNTY

My goodness . . . I do believe somebody has cut off my horse's head!!!

It is not known, for sure, when the Clear Creek Baptist Church, located on CR 428 between Flynn and Marquez, was formed. Apparently, in 1894, a fire destroyed all the church records. One of the charter members, Mrs. Winifred Asbury Seale, was quoted on her ninetieth birthday, in 1914, as saying the church was begun in 1852. This would make it one of the older churches in the area. The church—as is the community—is named for the creek that flows nearby.

Clear Creek Baptist Church

It is believed the first building was a log structure and was also used as a school. Among the early families were Allison, Copeland, Dowell, Fowler, Winn, Grimes, Hodges, Hines, Neyland, Phillips, Watson, Vestal, Seale, Richardson, and Dezell. Early deacons were Elisha Sparks, Wyatt Seale, John L. Grimes, Calvin Bennett, Isaac James Hodges, and Jeremiah C. "Coon" Phillips.

Although the records are incomplete, it is known that one of the early pastors was Rev. James Smiley Neyland, who organized and/or pastored so many of the early Baptist churches in that area.

"My earliest exposure to the Clear Creek Church was as a tiny baby, lying on a pallet on the floor" recounts Mrs. Middie (Payne) Hoke. "I grew up in that church . . . Rev. Smiley Neyland was my great-grandfather. I can remember riding in our wagon to go to church on Sunday. Finally, when I was eleven years old, Daddy bought a car. I was baptized in a little branch, nearby—in dirty water—I'm not sure what year it was. I joined the church when I was fifteen. We moved away when I was seventeen, but we later moved back."

Mrs. Hoke recalls stories of one particular pastor—we'll call him Bro. Smith (not his real name)—who was a somewhat unusual man, to say the least. "Bro. Smith was considered a good, Christian man—and a good preacher—but he was sort of absent minded and was a little bit peculiar . . . in fact, he was a whole lot peculiar. I remember my mother telling about one Sunday when Bro. Smith ate dinner with them . . . and he ate nothing but berry pie for the entire meal . . . three big platefuls. She remembered him asking politely 'Mz. Neyland, I believe I'll have another plateful of that berry pie, please ma'am.'

"Bro. Smith always rode to church on his horse. One Sunday, while he was preaching, some of the boys slipped outside, took the saddle off his horse and reversed it—putting it back on backwards. After church, Bro. Smith came outside, got on his horse, sat there in the saddle for a moment or two, and then offered this observation, 'My goodness, I do believe somebody has cut off my horse's head!'

"Bro. Smith's wife, Hancy, always rode behind him, on the same horse. She would use a block to stand on, to make it easier for her to get up on the horse. One Sunday, after church, Bro. Smith got on his horse and rode away, leaving Mrs. Smith standing there on the

block. Somebody yelled at him 'Bro. Smith, you left Hancy stand-ing on the block.' He reflected for a moment and offered this com-ment 'Well, I suppose one of the good brethren will take care of her,' and rode away. We have no record of what her reaction was."

The first church building burned—it is believed around 1870—and was replaced by a larger building. That structure served until 1950, when the present structure was erected.

Originally, the Clear Creek Church met only one Sunday per month, but in 1954, that was upgraded to two Sundays per month—and, since 1980, they have had services every Sunday.

Like most country churches, the Clear Creek Church has struggled at times, but now appears to be a strong and stable church, under the present pastor, Rev. J. R. Tapley. The church has a long history and rich tradition—and expects to live up to that his-tory and tradition for many years to come . . . even if they no longer have a block to stand on while mounting your horse.

Lone Pine Union Church

HOUSTON COUNTY

"It once served lots of folks."

It sits there now—empty and lonely looking—south of Crockett on CR 3410. It has been inactive for a number of years now . . . but the old Lone Pine Union Church was once a busy, thriving church.

Although it is not certain when the church was formed, it is known that it originally was a two-story building and served as both a church and a school.

According to Mrs. Beth Bitner, who is somewhat familiar with

Lone Pine Union Church

the history of the church, some of the early families were Milliken, Hairston, Mann, Haddox and Montgomery.

"As far as we know," says Mrs. Bitner, "the Lone Pine Church always functioned as a Union church. It was used by whatever congregation needed to use it. Somewhere around 1923, a new school was built. The top story of the Lone Pine building was then removed, and from then on, it functioned only as a church."

Because of its status as a non-denominational Union church, no one pastor preached here on a regular basis. Different preachers filled the pulpit, as needed, without regard to denomination.

Over the years, as other congregations built their own churches, the use of the Lone Pine building became more and more sporadic.

"Finally, about 1944, church services stopped altogether" Mrs. Bitner continues. "For a good many years, the building was used once a year for a homecoming service . . . but even that has stopped now. In 1977, the building suffered severe storm damage. It was repaired, and we think it's sound enough to last for a long time, yet.

"Who knows? . . . Population patterns may change and the church may be revived someday."

Evans Chapel Methodist Church

LEON COUNTY

Lots and lots of preachers.

In the mid-1880s, the residents of the Evans Chapel Community, between Leona and Flynn, decided they needed a church (and a school) of their own.

The first settlers had come into the area in the 1830s, but the heavy migration began around 1850, primarily from the "Old South" (Alabama, Mississippi, Tennessee, Georgia, etc.) and intensified after the end of the Civil War.

The Evans family was among the first families to settle here (coming from Alabama) and the community came to bear the Evans name. As the population grew, the need for a church—and a school—became evident. They decided to do something about it.

Mr. and Mrs. W. J. Cox donated land (along what is now FM 977) and sometime in 1886, the Evans Chapel Methodist Episcopal Church South came into being, with a cemetery next to it and a school building across the road. The church, according to the best information available, was built by W. J. Cox, E. F. Oden, W. C. Reed, and Alec and Ben Wynn (Author's note: W. C. Reed was my great-grandfather). The first pastor was Rev. Sam Vaughn.

The original building was used

W. C. Reed

27

Evans Chapel Methodist Church

until about 1919, when it was replaced by a new structure. That building is the one still in use today. Sometime later, when they needed new pews, the entire membership went out to Leon Prairie and picked cotton to raise money for the pews. As was common in those early days, the church was pretty much the center of the community—socially as well as religiously.

"I remember watching the smoke pour out of the building."

Mrs. Josephine (Cox) Murphy, ninety, is one of the oldest present members. "We lived within sight of the church" she recalls. "So, we usually walked to church. My daddy was a Methodist but my mother was a Baptist—and sometimes I sort of got caught in between. I didn't join the church as early as some of the other kids—but I finally joined—and I've been a member ever since."

Mrs. Josephine (Cox) Murphy

The church caught fire once, years ago, but the fire was put out without major damage. "I was just a kid" says Mrs. Murphy, "but I remember standing out in our yard and watching the smoke pouring out of the building. That made a big impression on me."

"I can remember seeing folks sitting in the open windows."

"I grew up in the Evans Chapel Church, says Rev. (retired) E. C. Phifer. I joined when I was eleven years old and I'm eighty-three now... so that was seventy-two years ago.

Rev. E. C. Phifer
—Photo courtesy of Rev. Phifer

"The church played a very, very important role in my early life . . . it helped shape my beliefs and values . . . and probably helped influence my decision to become a minister myself.

"I remember the revivals we had. Usually it was toward the end of July or early August—after the crops were laid by and before we started picking cotton. The weather would be real, real hot and the church would be full. Sometimes there wouldn't be enough seats for everybody. I can remember some folks sitting in the open windows. Other folks would sometimes complain that this interfered with the flow of air through the windows.

"One thing that I always thought made the Evans Chapel Church somewhat unique was that no one person—or family—was indispensable—or dominant. The leadership and responsibility was shared by a number of different folks.

"Money was always tight and I can remember lots of times, at the 4th Quarter Conference, the stewards would divide up and go out among the members, soliciting donations . . . trying to raise enough money to pay the preacher. They knew there wouldn't be any use trying to raise the money earlier . . . they had to wait till the farmers had their cotton crop picked and sold."

"I always had to clean the church."

Mrs. Johnnie Rae (House) Tisdale, at eighty-nine, is one of the older members of the Evans Chapel Church. "We lived right across the road from the church . . . so I was 'close to the church' in more ways than one" she recounts. "When I was just a kid, I had the job of cleaning the church every week. I started doing this when I was just barely big enough to hold a broom. There were others that helped out at times—Josephine Cox, Fannie Lamb and others—but because I lived so close, Mama sent me over there every week with my mop and broom.

"I remember one summer when we were in a terrible dry spell . . . the crops were burning up. A bunch of us went to the church to pray for rain. It started raining before we got home.

"The church was always so important to us. Back then it was the center of our community life—both religiously and socially."

"I don't remember joining the church."

Mrs. Betsy (House) Vann, eighty-one, is a sister of Mrs. Tisdale and also grew up in the Evans Chapel Church. "I don't actually remember joining the church" she says. "I was too young to remember it. We were having a revival and I was asleep on a pallet on the floor, up near the front. Some of the other girls—older that me—were in the process of joining. Mildred May woke me up, pulled me to my feet and led me up there to join. She was older than me . . . so I did whatever she told me to. The preacher didn't know what to do . . . but he finally went ahead and took me in. I guess he figured it couldn't hurt anything.

"I can remember watching Cousin Lon Hollingsworth cooking the big pot of stew, in a wash pot, when we had 'Cemetery Workings' . . . we always had dinner on the ground. Cousin Lon was an old man then, but he was very good at cooking the stew. He knew exactly how to season it . . . he always used squirrels for meat."

"Aunt Lou would stand up in the aisle and shout!!!"

Rev. Morris House (retired), eighty-five, grew up in the Evans Chapel Church, along with sisters, Johnnie Rae and Betsy—and their other siblings. "I vividly remember those summer revivals," he recalls. "They usually lasted two weeks and we would have services in the mornings as well as at night. One of the exciting events we always looked forward to was Aunt Lou Plotts's shouting. We would watch her as she 'got the spirit.' Aunt Lou would finally step

Rev. Morris House, Betsy House Vann, and Johnnie Rae House Tisdale
—Photo from author

out into the aisle, raise her arms and begin to praise the Lord! As I recall, she was the only 'shouter' in the church. Everyone called her "Aunt Lou" and we all loved and respected her. She taught the children's Sunday School class for many years.

"Lay members of the church were often called upon for the 'pastoral prayer.' There was one particular member who always said exactly the same prayer. It got to where the young people could recite his prayer, word for word.

"Every few years, the church would sponsor a singing school, where we were taught how to sing the old hymns, using a "Stamps Baxter Gospel Song Book." Periodically, different churches would hold an all-day—or Sunday afternoon—Singing Convention. These were very popular. I have very fond memories."

Today

The Evans Chapel Church today has a small, but fairly stable membership. It continues to have services on a regular basis, sharing a preacher with another small church (not an uncommon arrangement). Rev. Anthony Cecil is the current pastor.

The Evans Chapel Methodist Church claims (probably correctly) to have sent more of its members into the Methodist ministry (on a percentage basis) than any other church in the state.

There is no known reason for this—it just happened. In the House family alone, there are at least eight members that have become Methodist ministers. In the Lamb family, three of Charlie Lamb's sons became Methodist ministers and a fourth became a minister of another denomination.

In fact, the church has produced several Baptist ministers—and a couple who were of other denominations. No one is quite sure how that happened.

Even so, the Evans Chapel Methodist Church proudly claims all its ministerial progeny—regardless of denomination. This is a vital part of its legacy.

I Promise . . .

To join the Methodist Church today is a relatively simple process. Basically, you just have to promise, in front of the congregation, to support the Church and its teachings.

However, it has not always been that simple. In 1895, Fannie (Reed) House was eleven years old. (Author's note: Fannie (Reed) House was my grandmother.) Virtually all her life, she had been attending the Evans Chapel Methodist Church (at that time it was called the Methodist Episcopal Church South), and she decided it was time to make it official. On August 29, 1895, she joined. Her original Certificate of Membership has survived, even though it is somewhat fragile, and is reproduced here.

The pledge she had to sign was pretty detailed and didn't leave much to the imagination. To quote:

"I have assumed the following obligation: I renounce the "Devil and all his works, and the vain pomp and glory of the world, with all covetous desires of the same, and the carnal desires of the flesh, so that I will not follow or be led by them. I promise to be subject to the Discipline of the Church, and to attend upon its Ordinances, and support its Institution. All this I will Endeavor to do, God being my Helper."

Frannie Reed House

33

Not everything was simpler in the "Old Days." So far as I know, Grandma never violated the promises she made in that pledge.

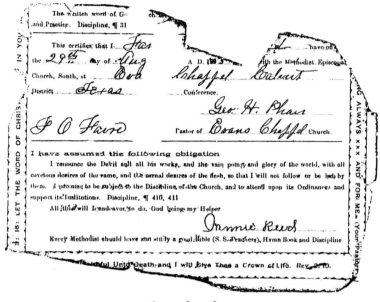

Copy of certificate

—From author

Reverend Z. N. (Wildcat) Morrell

"With nothing but my Bible, my hickory stick, and my rifle."

In any serious study of the history of the early development of the Baptist Church in frontier Texas, there is one name that shows up over and over—that of the Reverend Z. N. (Wildcat) Morrell. We have no formal, complete record of all the Baptist Churches he formed, but based on just the ones we know about, it is doubtful that anyone else approached his record.

Born in 1803, in South Carolina, and growing up in Tennessee (his family moved there in 1816), he became a preacher before he was fully grown. He preached in Tennessee for fourteen years, but began to suffer from health problems (it was described as "lung hemorrhages," but more likely was tuberculosis) and was advised to move to a warmer climate. He spent a year in Mississippi—forming three churches there—before moving on to Texas in April 1836. Actually, he had already preached his first sermon in Texas, in December 1835, while there on an exploratory trip.

Reverend Morrell initially settled at Falls of the Brazos, but because of Indian hostilities, he relocated to Washington on the Brazos and formed a church there

Rev. Z. N. Morrell

in 1837 (believed to be one of the very first Baptist churches in Texas). He performed his first Texas marriage, there in Washington, in the fall of 1837.

Over the years, in addition to his preaching, Rev. Morrell was involved in land speculating, merchandising, school teaching and politics (you couldn't make a living on preaching alone) but was not particularly successful in any on these activities. He never achieved any measure of financial security.

Records indicate that he fought in the Battle of Salado in 1842. It appears that Rev. Morrell was definitely not a pacifist.

In 1846, he was appointed as a missionary by the Domestic Mission Board of the Southern Baptist Convention, and made regular monthly trips, by horseback, from Cameron to Corsicana, a 300 mile round trip. Not surprisingly, this routine put a strain on both his health and his marriage

In 1867, he went to Honduras to do missionary work there, but because of health problems, returned to Texas two years later.

Rev. Morrell kept a dairy of his work and his travels and, in 1872, turned it into a book *Flowers and Fruits in the Wilderness, or 46 years in Texas and Two Winters in Honduras.* This is considered the first extended effort to record early Baptist history in Texas.

Among the churches formed by Reverend Morrell—the ones we know about—(in addition to Washington on the Brazos) were Little River, in Milam County, in 1849; Marlin in 1852; Gonzales (unsure of the year); Huntsville in 1844 (with eight members); Anderson in 1844 (with seven members); Springfield in 1846 (with six or seven members); and Leona (Leon County) in 1846 (with nine members).

Reverend Morrell was instrumental in founding the Union Baptist Association in 1840; the Colorado Baptist Association in 1847; Trinity River Baptist Association in 1848; the Leon River Baptist Association in 1858; the Waco Baptist Association in 1860; and the Lavaca River Baptist Association in 1877.

In his book, Rev. Morrell describes in detail the problems he faced and the hardships he had to endure. He states that when he arrived in Texas in 1836, the entire population of the Republic of Texas was estimated to be 30,000 Anglos, 3,470 Mexicans, and 14,200 Indians. He tells of crossing the Trinity River at Robin's Ferry and traveling on the Old San Antonio Road. He tells of his first baptism in Texas, "By request of the church I baptized Sister Dancer into the fellowship of the church . . . this was done about the first of March 1839, in the Colorado River, some eighteen or twenty miles above LaGrange, and was my first baptism in Texas. This was the first baptism that I have any account of west of the Trinity River."

He speaks of the desolation that existed in those days, "From LaGrange to Gonzales, fifty miles, there was but one house. From Gonzales to San Antonio, there was no house."

Rev. Morrell rarely had any measure of financial security. He tells of once crossing the Brazos River to visit Washington, "I had no money to pay the ferry . . . so I pledged my coat."

In those early days, Indians—particularly the Comanche—were a constant threat. Rev. Morrell mentions that the members always took their weapons to church. In fact, he stated that "There were three things that I always kept with me, no matter where I was— my Bible, my hickory stick, and my rifle."

It took him a full month to complete his circuit. He had to cross the Little Brazos River on every trip—with no ferry—he had to swim his horse across. In the winter he had to contend with numerous swollen creeks. He tells of one trip in 1846—he was on his way to Leona and Springfield and had to cross a creek that was deeper than he anticipated. His tired old horse got in trouble, and the Rev. had to get off the horse, into the water, to help his horse get out of the creek, onto the bank. The Rev. got completely soaked . . . it was the dead of winter . . . there was a "blue norther" blowing . . . it was 4:00 P.M. . . . and the next house was twenty-five miles away. But somehow he made it . . . he always did.

The Reverend Z. N. (Wildcat) Morrell died in Kyle in 1883, and was buried at the First Baptist Church there. In 1946, his body was moved to the State Cemetery in Austin. He left a rich legacy. Much of the growth and development of the Baptist faith in Texas can be credited to his efforts—and to his persistence.

Pageville Baptist Church

FORT BEND COUNTY

"Reverend Page had a vision."

Adam Page was born in 1810, in King George County, Virginia, as a slave. We don't know for sure when he came to Texas, but he was shown on the 1870 census as living in Harrisburg, Harris County, Texas, and was listed as a farmhand. It is likely that he migrated to Texas after the Civil War, as did so many Southerners—both White and Black.

We don't know for sure when he began his career as a minister. We do know that about 1880, the Rev. Adam Page organized and founded the Pageville Baptist Church, located at 4118 Clayhead Road, in Fort Bend County.

Mrs. Gertha Johnson
—Courtesy of Mrs. Johnson

According to Mrs. Gertha Johnson, a life-long member of the Pageville Baptist Church, "The story I was always told was that Rev. Page had a vision. Three times, the Lord told him, 'Adam, go build a house for the Lord.' So, Adam Page followed the dictates of his vision. He picked a spot there on Clayhead Road, north of Richmond, cut a sapling to mark the place and then knelt and prayed. Rev. Page, with the help of Rev. D. C. Smith, and others, cleared the site and built a church—a crude box-like building, with few windows or doors, and with benches instead of pews."

Rev. Page pastored the church until he died in 1903, at the age of ninety-three. He is buried there in the church yard, less than 100 feet from the front door of the church he founded.

Sometime in the early 1900s (we're not sure of the exact year) the original building was destroyed by a storm. The members constructed a new building on the same site. That building still stands and is still in use today. The building is unusual in one respect. Like many churches built in that era, it has twin steeples . . . but they are not the same. One steeple is about two or three feet higher than the other one. According to Mrs. Johnson, one of the steeples was built as a bell tower, and this accounts for the difference in height.

Many years ago, a major disagreement arose within the congregation. Some members, particularly some of the younger ones, wanted to move the church to a new location. The older members wanted to remain in the original location and their viewpoint prevailed. As a result, some of the members left the church and formed a new church, Mt. Olive Baptist Church, at a location a couple of miles away. A study of the old churches indicates this sort of dispute was not as unusual as one might think.

Pagevillle Baptist Church still functions on a regular schedule, under the leadership of Rev. John McClain, even though their mem-

Pageville Baptist Church.

bership is aging. Located in an area of tremendous growth, with new subdivisions springing up all around it, the church is facing all the problems created by urban sprawl, along with a steadily declining Black population. The present members, though few in numbers, have remained faithful and devoted to their "little church in the wildwood." Like so many other similar churches, however, they are facing problems—an aging membership, with not enough young members coming into the church to replace the older ones.

It is likely that the time will come, in the not too distant future, when the remaining members of the Pageville Baptist Church will have to make some difficult—and perhaps painful—decisions . . . the same kind of decisions that so many of the small country churches are facing. Hopefully, the church will continue to function for a long time yet to come. It has met the needs of its people for well over 100 years now. Rev. Adam Page, from his vantage point there in the front yard of the church, is no doubt pleased with what has transpired as a result of his vision so many, many years ago.

Rev. Page's tombstone.

Georgia Camp Baptist Church

HOUSTON COUNTY

"They leveled the building with mules."

During the period following the War Between the States, when so many "Old South" folks moved to East Texas, a group of these settlers from Georgia came to Houston County and camped for some time on the banks of a small creek (southeast of the present community of Austonio). They camped there for a good while before they got permanently settled. The creek became known as the Georgia Camp Creek and the surrounding community became known as Georgia Camp.

It is believed that sometime in the late 1870s, a Baptist fellowship was founded. For sometime, they shared a building with the Methodists—a not uncommon arrangement in those days. Early

Georgia Camp Baptist Church.

records indicate they erected their own building (a small building) in 1886. The present building (located on CR 3385) was erected in 1894. That building is still in use today.

Throughout the years, the Georgia Camp Baptist Church has always had a strong emphasis on music.

According to Mrs. Ruthie Elliott, "Some of the early families were Hester, Taylor, Wilcox, Nettles, and Kuhn. You can still find members of those families around here today. I'm ninety years old and I've been a member of the church for sixty-seven years. I've seen a lot of things happen in those sixty-seven years. I remember in the late 1940s when the southeast corner of the building got out of level. They levelled it by hooking a chain under the corner, running the chain over the top of the building and hooking a pair of mules and a pickup to the chain to raise the corner.

"We don't have many folks left any more, but we're still hanging on. We're down to ten or twelve people. Brother Earl Hester is our pastor. The church is still very important to us . . . it always will be, no matter what happens."

Mrs. Ruthie Elliott

Belott Penescostal Church

HOUSTON COUNTY

"We're determined to keep it going."

"I'm not real sure, but I believe the church was organized about 1940," says Mrs. Jean Walker. "I joined the church in 1945. I moved away for a few years, but I came back in 1979."

The Belott Pentecostal Church, a relatively small building, sits in a grove of trees on FM 1733, northeast of Crockett.

"Some of the early families that I can remember were Pyle, Vaughn, Ashmore, and McAnelly. Tom Duren, Mrs. McAnelly's father, gave the land for the church. The first pastor was, I believe, a lady, Rev. Jones. They worshipped under a brush arbor first, before they got a building up. We don't know, for sure, when the building was constructed."

Belott Pentecostal Church.

The numbers are low now, but the church still functions on a regular basis.

"Like so many of the small country churches, we're struggling now . . . we don't have many folks left . . . but those we have are strong and faithful. Our last pastor had some health problems and had to resign. We don't have a permanent pastor yet, but different people fill in. We still have services every Thursday and Sunday night.

"We're determined to keep it going . . . we just have to."

Leona United Methodist Church

LEON COUNTY

"Or was it Baptist . . . or maybe Presbyterian . . . or maybe something else?"

Few churches can claim to having begun life as a Baptist church and, over the years, evolving into a Methodist church. But that's the story of the Leona UMC—sort of.

Official records are somewhat sparse, but we know that along about 1845 or 1846, there were a few families living in Leon County, mostly around the Leona area, and they apparently felt the need for a church.

As far as is known, the only preacher active in the area then

Leona Methodist Church.

45

(Texas was still a republic at that time) was Rev. Z. N. (Wildcat) Morrell, a Baptist missionary/circuit rider/preacher who had been working in Texas since 1835. As was common at that time, these pioneer settlers welcomed any preacher they could get, regardless of denomination.

In his book *Flowers and Fruits in the Wilderness*, Rev. Morrell mentions the Leona church several times:

"My first trip across the middle country—Jan. '46—preaching at Leona and at Springfield . . . Second trip—Feb. '46—organized church at Leona with eight or nine members."

"Spring of '46—continued to preach at Leona on first Sunday of every month . . . had difficulty crossing the Little Brazos River and the Navasota River."

"Preached at Leona . . . then rode fifty miles to Springfield, preached there and then rode forty miles to Navarro County."

"First meeting at Leona after organization . . . a young slave named Jerry approached and asked to join the church . . . he said he was a believer . . . I baptized him . . . Jerry later learned to read the bible and I granted him permission to preach."

Records indicate the original members of the Leona church (Baptist) were: Robert Rogers, Alexander Patrick, Catherine

J. J. Pope.
—Author photo

Patrick, Elizabeth Childress, Delilah Rogers, Elizabeth Boggs, Cynthia Thomas, James Fowler, and J. J. Pope (Author's note—J. J. Pope was my great-great-grandfather).

It appears the church actually functioned as a "Union Church," serving three denominations— Baptist, Methodist, and Presbyterian—a not uncommon arrangement at that time. We have no record of when the Presbyterian congregation was formed. The earliest mention of Methodist activity in the county was in 1848, when Rev. Bryant J. Peel was assigned the Mission to Leon County, to begin the first of 1849. In 1851, Rev. Lewis

J. Wright was appointed as pastor of Leona Methodist Church. In those early years, services were held in the lower floor of a two room, two story building. The upper floor was occupied by the Masonic Lodge.

In 1885, the Methodist congregation constructed their own building, on a one acre site, near the old two story building. For the first time, the Methodists had a building of their own. They continued to use this building until 1928, when the present building was erected, on the same site.

At some point—we don't know when—the Presbyterian congregation disbanded, and later, the Baptist congregation relocated to a site on Leon Prairie, a few miles away, thus leaving the Methodist church as the only church remaining in the Leona Community.

The Leona UMC still functions today, as a small but fairly stable church, conducting services on alternate Sundays with the nearby Evans Chapel UMC (Rev. Anthony Cecil is the pastor). It doesn't seem to have suffered at all from having started out as a Baptist church—sort of.

Cedar Point Presbyterian Church

HOUSTON COUNTY

"I just wouldn't want to be buried anyplace else"

Mrs. Jeannette Creath Crell reflects on her relationship with the Cedar Point Presbyterian Church. "I'm ninety-six now, and I can't remember not being a member. I grew up in the Cedar Point church . . . I joined as a small child. Even though the church has been inactive for some years now, I still consider myself a member."

According to Mrs. Crell, the first Cedar Point church was built in 1885, a simple wood building constructed by the members. The church was rebuilt in 1957, using much of the wood from the original building. That building still stands on CR 1125, about twenty miles east of Crockett.

Mrs. Jeannette Creath Crell.

"There were only three Presbyterian churches in all of Houston County" says Mrs. Crell, "One in Crockett, one in Kennard, and ours at Cedar Point." Mrs. Crell has done extensive research on the history of the Cedar Point Church and reports it was organized by Rev. S. C. Alexandre, of Rusk, on July 26, 1885. The original congregation included members of the Creath, Brown, Yarborough, McCelvey, Baskin, McHenry, Ezell, Graham, Miller, and Merriweather families. The original Elders were J. W. Creath, J. S. Brown,

W. S. Baskin, and Dr. W. C. Miller. The original Deacons were J. W. McCelvey and C. M. Ezell.

The organizer of the church, Rev. Alexandre, served as the first pastor, for one year, and was followed by Rev. W. M. Kilpatrick, and then by Rev. C. C. Williams and Dr. S. F. Tenney. Mrs. Crell has fond memories of Rev. J. W. McCleod, of Rusk, who served as pastor from 1896 till 1924. "He would come all the way from Rusk in his buggy" recalls Mrs. Crell. "He would preach at Augusta, Kennard, and Cedar Point—on Friday, Saturday and Sunday. We referred to him as Old Man McCleod. We looked forward to seeing him drive up in his buggy."

"The Cedar Point Church was the center of our lives when I was growing up. Cedar Point has always been home to me—even though I was away for some years. I taught school for fifty-three years . . . for thirty-three of those years, I taught deaf children. I taught in Crockett, Huntsville, Hawaii and other places . . . but I always came home to Cedar Point."

Due to a declining population, the Cedar Point Church was dissolved in 1945—it was consolidated with the Kennard church. The building is still maintained by the Cedar Point Cemetery Association and is used occasionally for special events and for an annual homecoming in July of each year.

"Even though it hasn't been an active church for over fifty years now, I still think of it as my church" says Mrs. Crell. "I have a lot of memories there . . . and when I die, I expect to be buried there, in the Cedar Point Cemetery . . . I just wouldn't want to be buried anyplace else."

Cedar Point Presbyterian Church.

Good Hope Missionary Baptist Church

LAVACA COUNTY

"I've been a member for eighty-seven years."

"I joined the Good Hope Church when I was twelve years old ... I've been a member now for eighty-seven years." Morris Bedford—who does not look to be anywhere near his actual age of 99—was recalling the history of the Good Hope Missionary Baptist Church, located 2½ miles east of Hallettsville, just off Hwy. 90

Deed records show that the present site of the church was conveyed to the Good Hope Church—the trustees were Wm. Bedford,

Morris Bedford.

Caldwell Robinson and Louis Fitzgerald—in 1894 by Israel Williams. It is believed the church was actually organized in 1888— with eight members—and had been holding services under a brush arbor in those early years.

According to Mr. Bedford, the first building was very small and was constructed about 1907, with the present building being erected in 1937. Some of the early families were the Bell, Williams, McAfee, Foley, Godley and Bedford families.

"The year I was born— ninety-nine years ago—the church got its bell" recalls Mr. Bedford. "Up till then they had

50

been using a horn . . . you could hear that horn for two miles. The bell was donated by Mr. Gus Samitch, a Jewish man who lived in town. My daddy brought the bell out from town and put it in place.

"I still go to church every Sunday. For years I was a bible teacher . . . I teach part-time now. The church is still real important to me—and to the other members. We don't have as many folks as we used to. We used to have 100 or more members . . . now we have about forty. Rev. Dennis Herring is our pastor, now . . . we still have services every Sunday. The Good Hope Church has been a big part of my life for eighty-seven years . . . It will still be important to me for as long as I'm here."

Good Hope Baptist Church.

Beria Missionary Baptist Church

HOUSTON COUNTY

"We needed it—we depended on it—we leaned on it"

"I'm eighty-eight years old" says Mrs. Alberta Moore, "and I've been in the Beria Church for as long as I can remember. It's just always been there. It's always been a part of my life."

Records indicate the Beria Missionary Baptist Church was organized in 1867, by Rev. John Baldwin, Elder Coffee, and Elder Roe Field Cotton. (Author's note: Rev. Cotton's name shows up frequently in the histories of other churches in Houston County. In some instances his name is spelled Row Field. We don't know which spelling is correct). Early deacons and members were John David, Burrell Johnson (who gave land for the first church), Dock Jones, John Jones, and Jack Lee.

Mrs. Alberta Moore

The first church was built of pine logs. Elder Coffee became the first pastor. Rev. Cotton was the second pastor, and Rev. Martin Reese was the third. Among the early families were Brice, Richard, Arledge, Porter, Jones, and Johnson.

The first church was located about eleven miles east of Crockett, on the south side of Hwy. 7. The present site is about nine miles east of Crockett, on CR 1035.

It is not known when the first building was erected, but in 1908, under Rev. J. H. Woodall, the existing building was repaired and enlarged. In 1942, under Rev. J. H. Hill, the old church was torn down and rebuilt. In 1953, under Rev. B W. Nobles, that building was torn down and the present structure was erected. The ground for this sanctuary was broken by James Oliver Dubose, a great-grandson of Burrell Johnson, who gave the land for the first church.

Under the present pastor, Rev. Nathaniel Thacker, the church has services two Sundays per month. Membership is small. "We're down now to about six or seven reliable members," laments Mrs. Moore. "So many of the older ones have gone on in . . . and the younger ones have moved away. It's so sad. Although I raised two children, I was never blessed with any children of my own—and the Beria Church was like family to me. It was always there. We needed it—we depended on it—we leaned on it. We're going to hang on as long as we can . . . we just have to."

Beria Baptist Church.

Greater First Baptist Church of Anderson

GRIMES COUNTY

"It's still there . . . after 135 years."

Sometime in 1867, a group of former slaves in the Anderson area (Grimes County) decided they needed a church—so they organized one. According to information in "History of Grimes County," compiled and edited by the Grimes County Historical Society, they named it the Greater First Baptist Church for Black Citizens of Anderson. Later—we don't know just when—the name was shortened to simply the Greater First Baptist Church of Anderson.

It is believed the original church was organized by the

Greater First Baptist Church

Reverends Baines, Parton, Buffington and Stribbling. Services were held in the White Baptist Church on Sunday afternoons (this sharing of facilities was not as uncommon as many might think).

In 1869, for reasons that are unclear, the church was reorganized, by the Reverends Campbell, Venerable, and Rheihart. Alexander Terrell was the first deacon. Services were held in the courthouse. Early families included White, Stowers, Terrell, Kennard, Taylor, Keri, Lattimore, Turner, Minor, Mason, Campbell, Mitchell, and Washington.

It is not known exactly when the first church was built. It is known that, around 1875, they bought one half-acre of land in the edge of Anderson, on what is now Hwy. 90, and erected a permanent building. That building is still in use today.

Among country churches, this is one of the more striking in appearance. It is a rather large building, with a high steeple, located on the side of a hill, right by the side of Hwy. 90. It has a beautiful oak tree right in front of it and has a magnificent old church bell there in the church yard. It presents an attention-getting sight to anyone traveling on Hwy. 90.

"I grew up in this church" says David Dickson, Jr. "I'm the oldest deacon serving now. My daddy was a deacon before me. The church has been a very, very important part of my life, and the lives of the other members. We're smaller now than we used to be, but we've still got a solid, strong church—Rev. Bryce Walker is our pastor now. This church has been here for 135 years . . . we're going to still be around for awhile yet."

Brown Chapel United Methodist Church

LAVACA COUNTY

"I'm 90 years old . . . and I grew up in the Brown Chapel Church."

Located on a hillside on CR 217, northeast of Hallettsville, the Brown Chapel Methodist Church looks out over the surrounding countryside, just as it has for more than 120 years.

Although official records are scarce, it is known that Sidney Williams donated two acres for a church and cemetery in 1881. It is believed the church had already been formed—or was formed shortly thereafter—and the building was constructed soon after that.

Some of the early families were: Newton, Payne, Stevens, Williams, Dees, and Sampson.

According to Mrs. Pinkie Stevens Newton, "I'm ninety years

Brown Chapel Methodist Church

56

Mrs. Pinkie Stevens Newton.
—Courtesy of Mrs. Newton

old and I grew up in that church. Back then there were lots of people living in the community and we had a pretty big church membership. We had a very active church. The earliest preacher I know about was a Reverend Vance, but I don't know if he was the first one or not. It has always been my understanding that this is the original church building—the only one we have ever had. For many years, there was a school—the Eilers Industrial Training School—that operated at the same location, in a separate building. The congregation is down to just a handful of members now—so many folks have moved away or died off. But the church is still very, very important to us. We still have regular services—one Sunday a month (the present pastor is Reverend Zettie Woodson) and we do the best we can. No matter what happens, the Brown Chapel Church will always be very dear to me."

Union Chapel Baptist Church

HOUSTON COUNTY

"When the bell rang, we knew somebody had died."

"I've been a member of the Union Chapel Baptist Church all my life" says Sam Wagner, eighty-eight. "My family moved to this community (Hall's Bluff) when I was four, and I've been a member ever since. I became a deacon in 1951, and I've been one ever since—I'm Chairman of the Deacons now. There's only one other

Mrs. Georgia (Wagner) Murphy, Mr. and Mrs. Sam Wagner, and Mrs. Murphy's grandson—representing three of the family generations involved in the church.

deacon now—my grandson, A. L. Murphy, Jr. My daughter, Georgia Murphy, is the church secretary. This church has always been a very important part of our lives. I think the same thing would be true for most of the folks that grew up around here."

The Hall's Bluff Community, located about fifteen miles west of Crockett, had its beginning about 1867, when Joshua Hall moved there, bringing with him a large number of black farm workers, and established a big plantation. In 1876, others migrated into the community from Mississippi, Missouri, and Maryland.

Almost immediately, the black settlers began to have worship services, wherever they could, on a somewhat informal basis. Eventually, Joshua Hall's daughter, Mrs. Banda Hall Halliard, donated a piece of land for worship purposes, and a brush arbor was erected. Rev. Rowfield Cotton, a traveling circuit preacher, conducted services.

In 1887, the church moved into its first building, a log cabin. In those early days, the church was called St. Daniel Church, and functioned as a union church, serving all denominations. The first pastor was Rev. George Manns. Deacon William Ward was one of the church leaders in those early days.

It is unclear when the present building was erected, on the side of a hill in a thick grove of trees, but in 1906, it was remodeled. At this time, one of the members, Elizabeth Ward, purchased a church bell from Sears and Roebuck. Earl Mitchell and Jim Benton were the first sextons, in charge of the bell. As was the custom with most old country churches, the bell was used to announce services on Sunday—and, at other times—to inform the community of a death.

"If we were working out in the fields" recalls Deacon Wagner, "and we heard the bell ringing, we knew somebody had died. We would stop whatever we were doing and walk to the church, to find out who had died."

According to the church history, compiled by Secretary Georgia Murphy, in 1909, under Rev. Andrew Mitchell, the St. Daniel Church became the Union Chapel Baptist Church. Other early pastors were Rev. Alfred Reese, Rev. King Mitchell, Rev. Bob Groves, Rev. Burnett, Rev. Fischer, Rev. Lemon, and Rev. D. S. Bailey.

Sometime in the late 1920s, the church was remodeled. "I was in school, across the road at the Salt Branch School" recalls Deacon

Wagner, "and, for two years, I could hear Mr. Monroe "Sun-Man" Dickson working on the church. I never knew why they called him "Sun-Man," but he worked hard, all by himself, off and on for two years, fixing up the church."

In 1949, under Rev. W. D. Dowes, the church was remodeled again.

Later pastors at the church included Rev. J. T. Grove, Rev. J. H. Hill, Rev. E. J. Jones, Rev. Young, Rev. Fleets, Rev. P. Gibson, Rev. Lusk, and Rev. Taylor. There have been a number of deacons over the years, including one, Deacon King Ward, who lived to be 106.

The Union Chapel Baptist Church is still there, on the side of that hill, there on CR 2065, It continues to function, on a regular basis, and remains a strong, stable church, under Rev. Elliott Marshall, the youngest pastor they have ever had.

Union Chapel Baptist Church.

Redland Missionary Baptist Church

LEON COUNTY

"We started with a Rev. Neyland . . . we've got a Rev. Neyland now."

Sometime in 1888, a group of seven people met in the Redland Community (so called because of the abundance of red soil there), a few miles west of Centerville, and decided to form a church. They called it the Redland Missionary Baptist Church. One of the founding members was Rev. James Smiley Neyland, a well-known Baptist preacher who lived in the area. Rev. Neyland was a circuit-rider, who, over the years, organized many Baptist churches in this portion of Texas. Although there is no written record to verify this, it is generally assumed that Rev. Neyland was the force behind the formation of the church, and served as its first minister.

The other six founding members were: Rev. Neyland's wife, Lucinda M. Neyland, their son, R. L. (Bob) Neyland, Mrs. McSheef, Cora Neyland, Laura Neyland, and R. Porter.

They now had a church . . . but they didn't have a building . . . and they wouldn't have one until almost twenty years later. They had services sporadically—whenever they could get a preacher there—under a brush arbor, in a school building, or wherever they could find a place to meet. Little history exists for this period of time—apparently, no minutes were kept. According to research done by Mrs. Jewel Posey and Mrs. Annie Wilkerson, however, it appears that, in addition to Rev. Neyland, other preachers that served the church during this time were Rev. E. R. Berry, Rev. T. H. Franklin, Rev. E. W. Parish, and Rev. Chase.

By 1907, their numbers had increased, and they decided they needed a permanent place to worship. Several of the men traveled to Bedias, by wagon, and brought back lumber. After a lot of hard

Redland Baptist Church

work, they had their building. Rev. T. H. Franklin was the first permanent pastor, R. L. Neyland was a deacon, and Mrs. Nettie C. Neyland was the first church clerk. They held their first revival in July of that year.

Rev. R. E. Sugart was the second pastor, and he was later followed by Rev. R. M. Hodges. A few years later, under Rev. E. E. Rogers, a split—or division—occurred within the church. The reasons for the split have long since been lost . . . and the church survived.

Sometime in these early years, according to Mrs. Grace Wall, the church had a pastor whose wife had a "hump-back." Some of the young boys in the church laughed at her. She, in their presence, started praying for the boys to develop a "hump-back." This immediately put a stop to the problem.

In 1928, under the leadership of Rev. W. D. Andrews, a new sanctuary was built and served until 1959, when the present structure was built.

Over the next forty years or so, the Redland Church functioned, on a regular basis, as a fairly strong country church. Then, in the 1970s and 1980s, the general decline in the rural population began to cause problems—as was the case with so many country churches. Finally, around 1990, the Redland Baptist Church ceased to operate.

It remained inactive, until, in 1997, a determined effort, led by L. C. Wall, Jr. (a great-grandson of Rev. Smiley Neyland) and his

Rev. Smiley Neyland.
—Courtesy of Leon County
Historical Society

Rev. Heath Neyland.
—Courtesy of Mrs. Neyland

wife, Grace, led to the resurrection—and re-activation—of the Redland Baptist Church.

The church has functioned continuously ever since, with what appears to be a stable—although small—congregation. They have regular services, every Sunday.

The present pastor is Rev. Heath Neyland, a great-great grandson of Rev. Smiley Neyland, the founder of the church. (L. C. Wall, Jr., a great-grandson, is a deacon). Rev. Neyland, thirty-six, grew up in the nearby Venetia Baptist Church, and is well aware of the history and heritage involved—both of the church itself, and of the involvement of his ancestors. Rev. Neyland's family—his wife, Angela, and their four children, J. D., Caleb, Ashton, and Chloe— are also active in the Redland Church.

It is anticipated that the Redland Baptist Church will continue to function for a long, long time. And—who knows—it just might be that the influence of Rev. Smiley Neyland will still be around for awhile.

Reverend James Smiley Neyland

"He could preach for hours . . . and usually did."

As was the case with so many of the early pioneers who contributed so much to the early development of Texas, James Smiley Neyland was not born in Texas. He was born October 2, 1838, in Amite County, Mississippi, to John Louis and Elizabeth Owens Neyland. He was named for a neighbor of the Neyland's, a lawyer named James Smiley. The Neyland family relocated to Louisiana, and later to Texas (first to Polk County and later to Angelina County).

At the age of nineteen, James Smiley—still living in Angelina County—married Lucinda Brashears.

James served in the Confederate Army during the Civil War. Shortly after the end of the war—around 1865—James moved his family to Freestone County. Sometime in the early 1870s, they relocated again to Leon County, in the Bowling Community. James farmed and taught school. Sometime in the late 1870s, he "heard the call," and began to preach—on a "fill-in" basis. On August 22, 1884, James Smiley Neyland was ordained as a Baptist preacher.

As was common at that time, he was a circuit preacher, traveling (by horseback or buggy) over a wide area, preaching at a number of churches. He did most of his work in East Texas, but is known to have traveled to South Texas occasionally. It is known that he conducted several revivals in Karnes County.

Rev. Neyland was often called upon to organize and/or preach the first sermon at a new church. In 1888, he organized the Redland Missionary Baptist Church, near his home in Leon County. This was his "home church" and he was one of the seven founding members.

Rev. Neyland apparently was a strong and forceful preacher . . . to say the least. In later years, some of his grandchildren recounted with fond memories that his "sermons would often last for hours. Once he started speaking, nothing could stop him. Church members would appear for Sunday morning services, and when twelve o'clock arrived, they would all gradually leave, go home for dinner, leaving Brother Jim speaking to an empty church-house. After dinner, everyone would go back, sit back down, and continue listening for a few more hours. No one ever dared ask him if he was aware of their leaving."

Rev. Smiley Neyland.
—Courtesy of Leon County
Historical Society

In an interesting sidenote, the present pastor of the Redland Baptist Church is Rev. Heath Neyland, a great-great grandson of James Smiley Neyland. A great-grandson, L. C. Wall (along with his wife, Grace) is one of the lay leaders of the church.

In 1921, after a long and productive life serving humanity—and his Lord—James Smiley Neyland died at Redland. He is buried at Centerville. It is safe to say that James Smiley Neyland truly left his mark.

Augusta Union Church

HOUSTON COUNTY

"It served everybody."

There is a great deal of uncertainty regarding the date of origination of the Augusta Union Church, located east of Grapeland, on CR 1560. Some theories hold that it was built around 1840, with slave labor, by Rev. Russell Wilson, a Christian preacher. However, there is no documented evidence to support this. The problem is further complicated by the fact that the Houston County courthouse burned, sometime around 1865, destroying all deed records prior to that date.

According to Mrs. Shirley Cutler, who has done extensive research on the Augusta Church, "We simply don't know, for sure, when the church was built. It would appear that the Augusta settle-

Augusta Union Church.

ment had its beginnings in the 1850s. It got its first post office in 1857. The church building is the original structure, and it's built of sawn lumber. So far as we know, there wasn't any sawn lumber available in the community prior to the establishment, by a Mr. White, of a small water-powered sawmill on San Pedro Creek . . . and this appears to have been in the 1850s.

"The outside of the church is still pretty much the same as it was originally. The old bell is still there. We believe the bell was given about 1870 by a Mr. W. W. Davis," says Mrs. Cutler. "The bell was rung only for the beginning of a service or for some emergency."

Over the years , the Augusta Church was used by at least four denominations—Methodist, Baptist, Presbyterian and Christian. Prior to 1872, the building was also used as a school. In that year, a separate school building was built.

According to Mrs. Cutler, "The earliest record of the Christian Church use of the Augusta facility is of a marriage (James F. Williams to Louisa D. Helm), performed by a Rev. D. R. Wilson. Indications are that the Christian Church membership was never very large. It is not known when they ceased to have services."

The Presbyterian denomination is known to have used the Augusta Church as early as 1872. It is believed that a Rev. Samuel Fisher Tenney was one of the first—if not the first—pastor of the Presbyterian denomination.

The Baptist denomination used the Augusta Church at least as far back as the 1870s. On October 14, 1882, the 16th annual session of the Neches River Baptist Association was held at the Augusta Church. It is not known when the Baptist use of the Augusta Church ceased.

There is no record of the Methodist use of the church prior to 1900. One of the early Methodist pastors was a Rev. Arthur Williams. The Methodists were the last denomination to hold regular services at Augusta. According to Mrs. Cutler, the last regular services were held in the 1950s.

The building is used now for special occasions (weddings, homecomings, special meetings, etc.) It is used once a year for the annual meeting and homecoming of the Augusta Cemetery Association.

To quote Mrs. Cutler, "The Augusta church had several names, depending on which denomination was referring to it at the time—but the correct name is the Augusta Union Church. Although it had several names, and several denominations used it, the people worshipped only one God. Everybody attended church services every Sunday, regardless of which denomination was holding services that particular Sunday."

The Augusta Union Church still stands there . . . a symbol of and a tribute to those early settlers who suffered such hardships in those long-ago days.

Center Point Baptist Church

GRIMES COUNTY

"I plan to keep on preaching . . . and singing."

The Center Point Baptist Church, located off FM 1774, near Plantersville, is believed to be 155 years old. This would make it one of the older churches in Grimes County.

The church burned one Sunday morning in 1927, and with it all the church records. Rev. Carthorn Holmes was the pastor at the time. Under his leadership, they erected, on a temporary basis, a shelter—with just a roof and no walls. They held services there until they were able to build a replacement building . . . this is the building that is still in use today.

Rev. Tommie Lewis is the present pastor at Center Point. "I've preached at Center Point since 1991" says Rev. Lewis. We've usually got about thirty to thirty-five folks there . . . and we've got some

Center Point Baptist Church.

69

Rev. and Mrs. Tommie Lewis

young folks in the congregation. We have preaching once a month. We're pretty stable . . . we're holding our own."

As an interesting side-note, Rev. Lewis is a renowned gospel singer. "I've been singing for over forty years" he says, "with different groups over the years. It's something I've always enjoyed doing. As long as I'm healthy, I plan to keep on preaching . . . and keep on singing."

Coaxberry Baptist Church

GRIMES COUNTY

"The slaves worshipped and prayed in a thicket."

Most of the early history of the Coaxberry Baptist Church came from Mrs. Fannie Bradley, a former slave who died over fifty years ago, at the age of 108. She had come to Texas from Mississippi and lived just across the road from the Coaxberry Cemetery, with her twelve children, on what was then the Stoneham Plantation. Across the road from Mrs. Bradley's home was a thicket where slaves often gathered to pray and worship.

Some time after Emancipation, the plantation owners donated five acres of land for a church and cemetery. It is believed the church is named after the folks who donated the land. In 1886, the Coaxberry Baptist Church was organized. The present church building is the third one built there.

Some of the early pastors were Rev. L. Northington, Rev. Prince, Rev. Bailey, Rev. Brown, Rev. J. B. Barnes, Rev. L. K.

Coaxberry Baptist Church.

Williams, Rev. Jordan, Rev. Scott, Rev. Charlie Warren, Rev. Walton, and Rev. Walker.

Early deacons were Buster Shannon, Jack Green, Allen Marshall, Primus Marshall, Mammon Ward, Pat Debose, George Marshall, Rob Meachum, Jake Debose, Berry McMullian, and John Henry Gaston.

Rev. Tommie Lewis, seventy-five, has pastored the Coaxberry Baptist Church since 1976. "This is my home church . . . I grew up in the Coaxberry Church . . . I joined when I was nine" says Rev. Lewis. "After I got grown, I moved away and I drove eighteen-wheel trucks for forty-seven years. I started preaching while I was still driving trucks. I preached my first sermon at Coaxberry on Easter Sunday, 1976. I retired from driving trucks in 1989, and moved back here to Anderson. I preach at Coaxberry one Sunday a month and Center Point one Sunday a month. I've trained several other preachers while I've been at Coaxberry.

"Our congregation at Coaxberry is pretty stable . . . we usually have about eighteen to twenty folks there. We have a few young folks in the congregation. Our numbers are small, but we've got some good, solid Christian folks in our church.

"The Coaxberry Church means a lot to me. There are a lot of memories there for me. I hope I can still preach there for a long time yet to come."

Galilee–Living Hope Baptist Church

LEON COUNTY

"If you want me to preach for you . . . here's the deal!"

It's still there, sitting on top of a little rise, at the end of a lane, about 200 yards south of FM RD #977, between Leona and Flynn, in Leon County (East Texas). They don't have services there every Sunday now, but the Galilee—Living Hope Baptist Church is still in use, though its congregation is very small in numbers.

In appearance, it's not much different from many other old country churches. The star on the front gable end is a little unusual, but other than that, it's pretty much typical of small country churches built in that era. We're not sure, but we believe it was built sometime in the late 1920s or early 1930s.

It's beginning to show signs of its age—and the wear and tear

Galilee—Living Hope Baptist Church

that results from many years of regular use, but it appears to still be fairly weather-tight and solid.

What is different about the Galilee—Living Hope Baptist Church—what sets it apart from others—is its history—the story of its origin—how it came into being. This church owes its very existence to the dictates of one man . . . the Reverend Jefferson Norris.

In my earliest recollection of Rev. Norris (I grew up in the same community as he did), he was already an old man . . . but he didn't look it. He was one of those thin, wiry men who just don't seem to age. When he was in his nineties, he was still an active preacher. When he died in 1971, at the age of ninety-six, he was pastoring the Mount Calm Pine-Top Baptist Church (he had pastored this church for over fifty years).

Rev. Norris always credited his youthful appearance and manner to "Keeping busy . . . and doing the Lord's work." It sure seemed to work for him.

Born in 1874, the son of former slaves, Rev. Norris "heard the call" and began preaching when he was about thirty years old. Although he continued to farm (it was almost impossible to live on what you could make at that time as a country preacher), he began to preach and continued to do so for over sixty years, often serving two or more churches at the same time (this was not an unusual arrangement). In fact, Rev. Norris at times served as many as four churches simultaneously.

Usually this type of "sharing" arrangement worked out fairly well. However, on one of his charges, Rev. Norris began to run into a problem. He was serving two churches about two miles apart—the Galilee Baptist Church and the Living Hope Baptist Church. For reasons that have since been lost and forgotten, a great deal of bickering and petty jealously began to develop between the two churches.

It finally reached the point where Rev. Norris became so exasperated with the situation that he left and took on a different charge. A couple of years later, the two churches asked him to return. After much serious study of the matter, he agreed—on one condition. The two churches must combine into one—he didn't want a repeat of the previous problems. When he said they must combine into one church, that's exactly what he meant. He required them to physically tear down the two existing church buildings, haul the lumber to a new in-between location, and build a new church building. They did it . . . and thus was born the Galilee-Living Hope Baptist Church. This apparently solved the problem. Rev. Norris successfully pastored this new church for many years.

In fact, he pastored the church, in one form or another, for over fifty years.

Rev. Norris was a highly respected man in the entire community, throughout his lifetime, and he left a rich legacy—both as a man and as a minister. Of all the monuments and tributes to his life and to his ministry, perhaps none are as striking as the Galilee—Living Hope Baptist Church . . . a church that came into being because the Reverend Jefferson Norris decreed it.

Rev. Norris. Photo from funeral notice.
—Courtesy of Laura McLeod

(enter]ill Primitive Baptist (hurch

WALLER COUNTY

"We still observe the doctrine of the Primitive Baptist Church."

Located on Center Hill Road, east of Hwy. 6, between Hempstead and Navasota, the Center Hill Primitive Baptist Church was organized in 1882, when Abraham Simmons, Delum Toler and Henry Goodwine (the original Trustees) bought one acre of land.

Early pastors included Rev. John Harry Simmons, Rev. Bap Goodwine, Rev. Milo Wilson, Rev. Charlie Johnson, Rev. Ed Hill, Rev. Michael Todd, and Rev. Sam Davis. Early families included the Thompson, Goodwine, Brooks, Steptoe, Marshall, McKinney, Barnes, Bennet, and Yates families.

Rev. and Mrs. John Harry Simmons.

—Courtesy of Rev. Hayes

Center Hill Primitive Baptist Church

For many, many years, the Center Hill Church held services on only one Sunday per month, so the members could fellowship with other churches in the community, primarily St. Luke Baptist and Lawrence Key Methodist. This practice continued until 1995, when they began having services every Sunday. Throughout its history, the Center Hill Church has observed the traditional Primitive Baptist doctrine . . . namely Baptism, the Lord's Supper, and Foot Washing.

Unlike many of the older country churches, the Center Hill

Rev. John Harry Simmons
—Courtesy of Rev. Hayes

Rev. Richard Hayes
—Courtesy of Rev. Hayes

Church appears to be a strong, stable church . . . and is growing. Even so, the church still remembers its roots . . . and its traditions. The present pastor, Rev. Richard Hayes, (he has been the pastor since 1978) is the great-grandson of Rev. John Harry Simmons, one of the very first pastors. The oldest member of the church, Mrs. Willie Wilson, recently celebrated her 102nd birthday.

As Rev. Hayes puts it "We've been here a long time . . . but we've still got a lot of work to do, yet. We're going to be around for a long time to come."

Cedar Branch Missionary Baptist Church

HOUSTON COUNTY

"They pledged $20 each to pay for the church building."

In 1862, in the area west of Grapeland (on what is now CR 2210) a group of freedmen—former slaves of John and Ana Jane Pouncey Smith—decided they needed a place to worship. They erected a brush arbor along a little branch—there were lots of cedar trees there—and began to worship, on an informal basis. They had no pastor at this point. Some of the early families were the Leonard, Burns, Campbell and Price families.

In 1864, they erected their first building—a very small building. It is believed the original members, at this point, were Charles Leonard, Alonzo Campbell, Henry Pouncey, Harry Rufflin, Levy Leonard, Monna Price, Comfort Campbell, and Addis Pouncey. They named their church Cedar Branch. In those early days, much time, particularly in Sunday School, was devoted to simply teaching the members how to read.

In 1895, they built a second building—they felt the need now for a larger facility. Members who pledged $20 each to pay for the building were Joe Bell, Tom Leonard, Jim Burns, Levy Leonard, Doc Campbell, Charles Leonard, Alf McLean, and Earnest Burns. Although by today's standards, $20 seems inconsequential, in 1895 that was a lot of money. One of the guarantors, Earnest Burns, died before he had a chance to pay his pledge. Another member, Snap Warfield, paid it for him. The pastor of the church at this time was Rev. E. L. Brown.

In 1924, the third structure was erected. This building still serves today. Larger than most old country churches, it is an impressive looking structure. The pastor at that time was Rev. R.

79

Cedar Branch Baptist Church

Harvey, and the deacons were Charles Leonard, Alf McLean, Josh McDaniel, B. W. Burns and French Harper.

"I grew up in the Cedar Branch Church . . . I'm a deacon now" says Hubert E. Burns. Five generations of my family have been involved with this church. My great-grandfather, Jim Burns, was one of the original trustees of the church. He was one of those who pledged $20 to pay for that building in 1895.

"My father, Hubert Lee Burns, was a trustee. My children were all baptized in the Cedar Branch Church and were members till they grew up and moved away.

"We don't have as many members as we used to . . . but we've still got a strong, stable church. The other deacons are Larry Leonard, Herman Tryon and George Ray Pierson. Our pastor is Rev. Frankie Jackson, and he preaches on the second and fourth Sundays of the month. We're proud of our church . . . it's important to us . . . and it always will be."

Stoneham Methodist Church

GRIMES COUNTY

"It rose from the dead."

In 1892, Rev. J. C. Mickle (Presiding Elder) organized the Stoneham Methodist Church, in the Stoneham Community, east of Navasota. There were twelve charter members. In 1893, according to deed records, Joe Stoneham donated land for a church, and the church was built the following year. Throughout the history of this church, the Stoneham family (through several generations) has been intimately involved with the church.

Frances Stoneham compiled much of the information regarding the history of the church. According to Mrs. Stoneham's findings, published in *The History of Grimes County*, the first pastor was Rev.

Stoneham Methodist Church.

R. W. Adams. The Sunday School was organized in 1894 by David Stoneham, who served as its superintendent for over fifty years.

In those early years, the Stoneham Church functioned steadily and was a strong church with a relatively large membership. In later years, however, as rural populations declined, the church began to suffer, and, finally, in 1960, it closed.

The church remained inactive until 1973, when a small, but determined group of citizens, led by John Mulholand, decided to reactivate the church. Finally, on September 30, 1974, the opening service was held . . . and the Stoneham Methodist Church was once again alive and well. The building was renovated and remodeled, and the church has functioned steadily ever since.

Under the leadership of the present pastor, Rev. Roger Goldsmith, the Stoneham Methodist Church holds regular services and continues to function—a church that literally died and was resurrected.

Greater New Hope Baptist Church

HOUSTON COUNTY

"We had Jack-leg preachers in those early days."

In 1930, a group of folks in the Daly Community, west of Grapeland, decided they needed a church of their own. Prior to that time, they had been worshipping at the Shepherd Masonic Hall, courtesy of Mr. H. W. L. Shepherd.

John Taylor and Spencer Stubblefield took the lead in getting the church organized. Mr. Balis Daly donated land for the church— and they were in business. The entire group joined in the effort to raise enough money for the building. They hired two carpenters, Mr. Virginia Walker and Mr. Ben Shepherd, and the first building became a reality. The pastoral minister was Rev. Peppy Reese. The deacons were Henry Wilmore, Isaac Stubblefield, Earnest Isadore, Elmo Stubblefield, John Taylor, and Spencer Stubblefield.

Mrs. Alice Shepherd.

Among the early families were Shepherd, Stubblefield, Howard, Hicks, Murphy, Burns, Gilford, Thompson, Taylor, Marshall, Denby, Benjamin, Isadore, Wilmore, Jackson, and Johnson. In the early days, the New Hope Church used many "Jack-leg" preachers. There were two kinds of preachers in those days, according to Mrs. Alice Shepherd, a life-long member of the church. "The preachers that had a permanent church were called 'Big Preachers'—and those that preached wherever they could were called

83

Greater New Hope Baptist Church.

'Jack-leg Preachers.' It wasn't till later that we were able to get a 'Big Preacher.'"

The present building was erected in 1943, and still serves today, there on FM 227, under Rev. J. L. Moten, who has pastored the church for the past thirty-seven years.

Says Mrs. Shepherd, seventy-nine, "The church was always a very important part of my life—and it still is. We only have services once a month now, and our numbers are small—but we're still hanging in there. We don't have many young folks . . . they've all moved away . . . but to those of us that are left, the church still means a lot to us."

Author's Note: I interviewed Mrs. Shepherd—and took her photo—in December 2002. On January 22, 2003, Mrs. Shepherd died. On January 25, Mrs. Alice Shepherd was "sent on home" from the Greater New Hope Baptist Church, the little church she loved so dearly.

Hillary Chapel Methodist Church

LEON COUNTY

"I joined the Hillary Chapel Church about 1913 or 1914."

"I joined the Hillary Chapel Methodist Church about eighty-eight to ninety years ago" says Mrs. Willie (Washington) Lankford, ninety-four. "I was born in 1908 and I think I was about five or six years old when I joined. I've been a member ever since. My parents, Mr. and Mrs. Sid Washington, and my grandmother, Texana Manning, were members of the church before me."

Two of Mrs. Lankford's uncles, Willie Washington and Forney Polk, were early trustees of the Hillary Chapel Church. The early history of the church is somewhat sketchy, but it is believed the church was founded by a Rev. Hillary, sometime in the late 1800s. It is believed Rev. Hillary was probably the first pastor. Located

Mr. and Mrs. Roger Lankford.

—Courtesy of Mrs. Lankford

Hillary Chapel Methodist Church.

about a mile west of Leona, just off FM 977, the Hillary Chapel Methodist Church has functioned continuously ever since. Sometime in the 1930s, the present building was erected.

"In 1931, I married Roger Lankford. Roger grew up in the Spring Creek Community and had been a member of the church there. In 1932, Roger transferred his membership to Hillary Chapel, and—like me—he's been a member ever since. Roger's one hundred and four now, and is the oldest member of the church."

"The church was always so important to us. Back then, we always had lots of social activities at the church. For years and years, Roger and I walked to church. We didn't get our first pick-up till many years later. Sometimes we would go in the wagon . . . but most of the time, if the weather was okay, we would walk. We're both kinda stove up now, and we don't get around as good as we used to—we have to depend on somebody else to take us to church—but we go when we can."

Like so many of the old country churches, Hillary Chapel is struggling to maintain its membership. They have services two Sundays per month, under the leadership of the present pastor, Rev. Carey Cauley, Jr.

"Our membership is small now . . . so many of the older ones are gone . . . and there's not many young ones coming along to take their place. But the church is still very, very important to those of us that are left."

High Point Baptist Church
Grimes County

"He says as long as there's one person there, he'll come and preach."

The early history of the High Point Baptist Church is very sparse—all the records were lost when the first building burned about 1927. It is believed the church was originally organized sometime in the mid to late 1860s. It is located on CR 308, in the Stoneham Community, east of Navasota.

According to Mrs. Glendora Connelly, a lifelong member of the church, "I always understood the first pastor was a Rev. Rhinehart. I'm seventy-five years old and I've been a member since I was a child. The church was always an important part of our lives. I can remember the revivals we always had. Lots of people would come,

High Point Baptist Church.

from miles around, to attend those revivals. Sometimes they would last for two or three weeks.

"Back then, we had a strong church with lots of members—but so many of them have gone on in, or moved away. We're down now to about four members, but we still have services on the third Sunday of every month. Rev. Wilbert Sargent is our pastor. He says as long as there's one person there, he'll come and preach."

Pennington Chapel Church

HOUSTON COUNTY

"I'm one of the original, charter members."

"I don't know for sure what the year was—I think it was in the late 1930s—but my father-in-law gave the land for the Pennington Chapel Church" recalls Mrs. Milo Pennington. "I knew some of the early families, but so many of them are gone now."

Located on CR 2245, west of Grapeland, the Pennington Chapel Church is somewhat distinctive in appearance, with the two small crosses located on the front of the building.

Fred Jones is one of the original members. "I'm eighty-one years old now," he says, "and I've seen lots of changes. I was a member of the old Arbor Church, not too far away. There was a split—a division—that developed within the membership. It finally got so

Fred Jones.

bad that seven of us left and formed our own church. We started worshipping first under a brush arbor, in the spring. In the fall, we put up our building. We called it the Pennington Chapel Church. The first pastor was a Rev. Weaver, from Elkhart. Some of the first families were Coleman, Shepherd, Lott, Robinson, Warfield, Burns—and my own family (Jones).

"Of those seven original members, there's only two of us left now—myself and Mrs. Rena

Pennington Chapel Church.

Burley. All the rest have gone on in. Over the years, I've seen six different pastors come through here. Rev. J. L. Motten—he's eighty-six—is our pastor now.

"We're small now, but we're still active. We have services two Sundays a month. It's tough when so many folks die or move away—but we're hanging on—we've got to—we just can't give it up."

First Baptist Church of Bedias

GRIMES COUNTY

"After 140 years, it still sits there, on top of the hill."

Located on a hilltop, just east of Bedias (Grimes County) at 22642 FM 2620, the old First Baptist Church building is believed to be the oldest still standing church building, of any faith, anywhere in the area.

This church was instrumental in the organizing of several other Baptist churches in the area—among them Mt. Pleasant, Enon, Pankey, and possibly others. Most of the available information on the church comes from *History of Grimes County*, compiled and edited by the Grimes County Historical Society.

The church is believed to have first been organized in 1848, by Reverend Anderson Buffington (he had fought in the Battle of San Jacinto). The first services are thought to have been held in a school building located on Simes Creek. During the next few years, they met in any place they could get. Then, in 1859, they bought land from W. C. Bullock, for $5, to be used for a church and cemetery. The church building was erected in that same year. Much of the work on the building was done by one of the members, C. J. Kerr.

As was common at that time, the church building was also used as a school.

For reasons that are unknown, there are no existing records of the church for the period of 1859 to 1913. It is believed that the membership never exceeded 200—it was never a large church.

Sometime in the late 1890s, a split developed among the membership, based on various philosophical differences. Finally, in 1912, a sizeable part of the membership withdrew and formed a new church, the Bedias Baptist Church, closer to town. A study of old

First Baptist Church of Bedias.

church histories reveals that such splits and divisions were not particularly uncommon.

During the early 1900s, the church developed a tradition of great music. Singing Conventions were held regularly and attracted visitors from miles around. That musical tradition continued for the life of the church.

The church continued to serve the community and the people, well, for many years. Finally, in the 1950s, the church began to suffer the fate of so many rural churches. The migration of so many, many people from the rural areas to the cities began to deplete the population—and the membership rolls.

Eventually, around 1965, there were so few members left, they simply couldn't carry on any longer—and services ceased.

The building has been restored—at least enough to preserve it—and it has been designated as a historical site.

Although now silent, the old First Baptist Church of Bedias still sits there, on top of the hill, as a reminder of all the people that have passed through its doors over the past 140 plus years—and the effect it had on their lives. It reminds us of days gone by—and the way things used to be.

Concord Missionary Baptist Church

LEON COUNTY

"We're going to get it going again."

On April 21, 1855, the Concord Missionary Baptist Church officially came into being, organized by Rev. W. A. Walker (he became its first pastor). The charter members were John Allison, Mirandy Moon, Willis Burkhalter, and Gerzilda Burkhalter. The land for the church was donated by Isaac Burleson, and the deed was recorded in 1856. U. T. Asberry was the first deacon. Located on a high hill, on Hwy. 7, between Centerville and Marquez, it is one of the oldest churches in Leon County, and one of the oldest churches in the Trinity River Baptist Association.

Records do not indicate when the present building was erected, but we know that in 1946, when Hwy. 7 was built, the building was moved to its present location so that it would be on the same side

Concord Baptist Church.

93

of the new highway as was the cemetery. There is no record of how it was moved, but it seems likely that it was moved by putting logs under it and hooking mules to it—that was a common way of moving buildings in those days.

Mrs. Edith (Burke) Lagrone has done extensive research on the history of the Concord church. "I've been a member of the Concord Church all my life" she states, "and my mother, Bertha Burke, was a member before me. The church was a big part of our lives . . . it was very, very important to us."

According to Mrs. Lagrone, some of the early leaders of the church included Jim Mattison, Conner Walker, Virgil Selman, G. B. Selman, Pleas Bull, Willis Willett, and John and Laura Powell. Records indicate that Mrs. Powell joined the church in 1875, and remained a member the rest of her life. Other long-time families within the church include: Winchester, Payne, Seale, Evans, Burkhalter, Grubbs, Yarborough, Simpson, Eddins, Little, Barrett, Burns, Springer, Burleson, Leavels, and Burdette.

Mrs. Lagrone recalls conversations with Miss Cora Kay (she joined the church in 1906 and was baptized in Buck Creek by Rev. Smiley Neyland) in which Miss Kay reminisced about riding to church on a horse, with her father. She recalled the Sunday afternoon "Church Conferences" after preaching was over, when the church leaders would "prefer charges" against members for dancing, fighting, cursing, gossiping, getting drunk, and other transgressions. Sometimes, members would be kicked out of the church for these transgressions—sometimes they would be cleared of the charges—and sometimes they would acknowledge their failings and ask for forgiveness.

In an interesting side-light, records of the Trinity River Association show that in 1880, the Concord Church paid their minister $125 for the year . . . in 1920, they paid him $32.50.

The Concord Church was a strong church for many years, until, in the late 1940s the dwindling rural population began to cause some problems. For a number of years, the church operated on a reduced schedule. Then, in the 1970s, the church became somewhat revitalized and went back to a regular schedule, under the leadership of Rev. Charles Pruitt. In addition to the regular services, the Concord Church, every year, on the Saturday before Easter, sponsors a big, big Easter Egg hunt that attracts many, many people. Also, once a year, the church has a Cemetery Memorial Service. This is an all-day service, with preaching and dinner-on-the-ground. Many of the folks who have moved away "come back home" for this event. "It's sort of like a homecoming."

In recent years, membership again began to decrease, and, at the same time, Rev. Pruitt's health began to fail. About a year ago, Rev. Pruitt died, and the church hasn't had a full time pastor since.

"Rev. Pruitt was such a good man—and such a good preacher— it was such a blow to us when he passed away" laments Mrs. Lagrone. "We just haven't been able to replace him. But we're still trying and we hope to get back to having regular preaching services at least once a month . . . in the meantime we will carry on."

Tadmor CME Church

HOUSTON COUNTY

"Or was it Bethel CME? . . . Or was it something else?"

Like many other old country churches, the Tadmor CME has not always had its present name . . . and has not always been located at its present site—there on CR 1135, just off FM 227, northwest of Ratcliff. It is believed the first church was located on the north side of Hickory Creek, about three miles from the present site, and it was called Bethel CME. It is not known when the church was first organized.

In 1894, the church—still known as Bethel CME—relocated to its present site. The new building was dedicated in 1900. The pastor, at the time, was Rev. R. W. Henderson. Early families included Johnson, Washington, Patton, Shepherd, Henderson, Franklin,

Carl Franklin

Mrs. Carl Franklin

96

Scott and others. The Tadmor community got its somewhat unusual name from the bible. In the late 1880s, the community was about to get a post office . . . so it had to have a name. The name "Tadmor" was suggested by a very devout Christian lady, Miss Kate Baskin. There were at least two biblical references to a "Tadmor in the wilderness" . . . and, as Miss Baskin put it "This place sure is in the wilderness." So . . . "Tadmor" it became.

It is not known when the Bethel church became the Tadmor church. Mr. Carl Franklin, eighty-nine, lives directly across the road from the church and, along with his wife Lucille (Henderson), eighty-four, has been a member all his life. According to Mr. Franklin, "The name change sort of took place gradually. There was a Bethel Baptist Church not too far away, over towards Ratcliff, and folks were always getting the two of them mixed up. Folks would call our church "the Tadmor church" . . . and over a period of time, that's what it became."

"I can't remember not being a member of the Tadmor church" says Mr. Franklin. "Except for World War II, when I was in the Army, I've always been here, and the church has always been a big part of my life. My parents were members before me. There used to be a school right next to the church and I went to school there."

L. K. Patton, ninety-five, also lives right across the road from the church, and also is a lifetime member—along with "my parents before me."

Both Mr. Patton and Mr. Franklin agree on the very, very important role the church has played in shaping the lives of the folks who grew up in the church. "I can't think of a single person who grew up in this church that ever got in any serious trouble with the Law" reflects Mr. Franklin. "They were taught right and wrong here . . . they were taught values. They were taught how to behave . . . and it worked. None of them ever got sent to the Pen—or got into any real trouble."

Mr. Patton agrees. He adds "This church, over the years, has turned out lots of preachers and teachers."

L. K. Patton

Tadmor CME Church.

Unlike so many of the old country churches, this one has never burned. "One time we had a fire that broke out in the ceiling, where the flue from the wood heater went through the ceiling" reflects Mr. Franklin. "But it happened while we were having services. When the fire broke out, there was a member down on his knees praying. He never missed a beat. He shouted 'Lord, please help us put out this fire. Amen!!' . . . and he jumped up and helped fight the fire."

The present building was built in 1962. Both Mr. Franklin and Mr. Patton were stewards at the time. "We don't have near as many folks as we used to" says Mr. Franklin. "So many of the old ones have gone on in and the young ones have moved away . . . but we still have preaching two Sundays a month, and once a year—in October—we have a Family and Friend Day, when lots of folks come back home."

"We usually have about thirty or forty folks at preaching . . . Rev. Johnson is our pastor now.

"This church is still important to us old folks . . . just like it has always been."

Elwood Methodist Church

MADISON COUNTY

"Some hard-working hens paid for the new pews."

One of the earliest communities in what is now Madison County was called French, in the vicinity of the Old San Antonio Road, near the intersection with what is now FM 1119. At some point, believed to be sometime in the 1840s, the settlers of French formed a church. As was common in those early days, the church (a log cabin located near the present Elwood Cemetery) served all the settlers, regardless of their individual denominations.

Sometime in the mid 1800s . . . probably in the late 1840s or early 1850s . . . things changed. The church became a Methodist Church, and has remained so ever since. During that same period, the community also changed. It was no longer called French. Instead, it became Elwood . . . maybe. According to Pat Wakefield,

Elwood Methodist Church.

99

a lifelong resident of the area, it was first known as Elmwood. This was due to the many elm trees in the community. In the adjacent community (known as Tanyard) there was a tanning yard, where, for several years, hides were tanned. The bark of elm trees contained a high level of tannin, a substance necessary in the tanning process. This was apparently a significant factor, at that time. According to Pat, over the years, the name was shortened and it became Elwood.

Later on, as the population of the area grew, a new building—an all-purpose building—was built, adjacent to the present cemetery. It was used as a school, fraternal lodges, a church for all denominations, and for just about any other purpose deemed necessary. The deed, dated in 1874, called for the land to be used "for school and church and graveyard privileges."

In 1897, the Methodist congregation bought a separate site, a little ways south of the cemetery. In 1899, they erected the present building. That building is still in use today. In 1928, they decided they needed more comfortable pews, but they had no money to buy them. The ladies of the church came up with a plan. They took all the eggs they collected on Sundays, and sold those eggs, with the money being dedicated to the fund for new pews. Due to these resourceful ladies . . . and due to some hardworking hens . . . they finally got their new pews.

The Elwood Methodist Church has functioned, continuously and without interruption, ever since 1897, and continues to function today, under the leadership of Rev. Richard Crosson.

Located on the church grounds is what may possibly be the world's smallest cemetery. It contains one tiny grave—that of "Little Becky Roberts, Daughter of J. O. and Maggie Roberts, born Dec. 8, 1900, Died Sept. 8, 1902." It seems that the family had lived in the community at one time, but had moved away. When the child died, they shipped the body back by train, with a request to bury her at the church. They didn't know that after they had moved away, the church had been moved and was no longer adjacent to the cemetery. In keeping with their wishes, little Becky was buried on the church grounds, and the grave has been maintained and tended ever since, by the children of the church.

In 1981, the Elwood Methodist Church applied for designation as a historically significant site. That request was granted, and

Grave of "Little Becky Roberts"

today, there is a Texas Historical Marker in front of the church. The church has met the needs of its members . . . and of the community . . . for over 150 years—and expects to continue to do so for a long time to come. And, incidentally, there are a couple of elm trees located there.

Reverend Benjamin James Shanks

"The Lord's not done with me yet!!"

"They say I was born in Dewalt, Texas, on the 7th day of the 7th month, in the year of nineteen hundred and five. They say when I was one week old, my father passed . . . and a week later, my mother passed. My grandparents took me and raised me, at Thompsons, Texas. I never have known what caused my parents to die. Back then, sometimes folks just died . . . and nobody ever knew why."

This was the first time I had ever actually met Reverend Benjamin James Shanks. I had known about him for some time. I knew he pastored the Zion Watchtower Missionary Baptist Church right down the road (FM 359) from where I live, north of Richmond, Texas, in Fort Bend County. I had been told that

Rev. B. J. Shanks

Reverend Shanks is possibly the oldest active preacher in Texas . . . if not in the entire country. I don't know if this is true . . . I couldn't find a list anywhere . . . but I think we can safely say there aren't very many ninety-seven-year-old ministers still preaching on a regular basis. In any case, it would be a very, very short list.

"We were always a church-going family . . . most folks were back then. We lived about two miles from the Mount Pilgrim Baptist Church there in Thompsons, and that's the

102

church I grew up in. My grandmother would take me in there and set me down right on the front pew, every time the church doors were open. We went to school in that same building. My schooling went through about the third grade . . . that's all the formal education I ever had. After that, I had to educate myself.

"Everybody worked hard back then—even the children. Every child had certain jobs and chores we were expected to do . . . that's just the way it was. If you didn't do your jobs you were in trouble. I spent my share of time in a cotton field when I was growing up. I didn't like it, but I did it.

"I first heard the call to preach when I was about five years old . . . but I didn't understand what I was being called for. Three times, I heard a voice that asked me 'Benjamin, what are you going to do when I call you?' It scared me to death . . . I didn't know what it meant.

"Nothing much else happened till I was about nine years old. Then I had a vision. The Holy Spirit appeared and spoke to me. The Spirit picked up a book and opened it. I saw my name in that book, in gold letters. The Spirit spoke, 'Benjamin, I have called you to preach.'

"Even though we were a religious family, there was still a lot I didn't know about religion at that time. I asked my sister to explain religion to me. She told me about Daniel and the troubles he had when he was a prisoner and was working for a king. She told me how Daniel prayed three times a day and maintained his religious beliefs, through all his troubles and trials. She told me to pray three times a day, and always keep my faith, no matter what might happen. I have always tried to do that ever since

"At that time, I considered myself converted, and a little later, when I was about ten years old, I was baptized in the Brazos River, right there near Thompsons . . . I could take you there and show you that exact spot today.

"I had mixed feelings about the call to preach. I resisted the "Call" for a long time . . . I just didn't feel like I could do it. But, at the same time I was resisting the "Call," sometimes I would get the urge to preach. When I would feel the urge, I would practice. I practiced on the animals. I would get the old mama dog and her puppies. I would tie her up so she couldn't leave—and I would preach to them. I would do the same thing to the mama cat, and to the milk cow, and to the pigs. It was a pretty good way to practice. They couldn't get up and walk away—and usually they didn't go to sleep. The only bad thing was I couldn't pass the collection plate around to them."

Still resisting the "Call," the young Benjamin Shanks finally decided it was time to leave the farm and get a job. "About the time I was good grown, I took a job as a section hand with the Sante Fe Railroad. I was still farming some on the side, but I kept this job for forty-four years, till I retired. Even after I started preaching, I kept this job . . . you couldn't make a living preaching back then. Working on the railroad was hard, hard work . . . and I was a small man, swinging a twelve-pound sledge . . . but I did what I had to do."

Reverend Shanks explained that this period of his life (in his twenties and early thirties) was not a good time for him. "I was still resisting the "Call" . . . I was still afraid of it. Things just didn't go well for me during this time. I got married and we had two children—and then, we divorced. My cows died—my hogs died—my crops failed. I was sickly most of the time.

"Finally, when I was in my thirties, I made some changes in my life. I accepted the "Call" and became a preacher, even though I still wasn't sure I was worthy. At that time the Holy Spirit appeared to me again and told me 'Since you accepted my call, I'm going to let you live way beyond 100 years.'

"I first started preaching in my home church—the Mount Pilgrim Baptist Church, in Thompsons. I remember my first sermon . . . I was so scared I was shaking like a leaf. My sermon was based on Isaiah, fifty-third chapter—the sheep before shearing and the lamb before slaughter. I didn't see how I was going to get through it—but, once I started preaching, my nervousness went away and the words came to me, somehow. I got through it okay."

Reverend Shanks served the Mount Pilgrim church until 1955, when he was called to pastor the Zion Watchtower Missionary Baptist Church. He has been there ever since—forty-seven years. Although he no longer preaches every Sunday, he still remains very active and usually preaches two Sundays each month. During this same period, he simultaneously pastored the Pleasant Hill Baptist Church in Fulshear for twenty-eight years.

Asked if, in all his years as a preacher, he ever had doubts about what he was doing, and whether or not he was "up to the task" Reverend Shanks replied, "Sure I have . . . and I still do . . . all the time. But, you just have to do the best you can—and keep your faith. The Lord will help you get through it. He will give you the strength and the wisdom you need to do what you have to do."

Reflecting on his long career, Reverend Shanks expressed one regret, "I wish I had kept a record of all the folks I have baptized, all the couples I have married, and all the folks I have buried. There is no telling how many there have been."

Asked about changes he has seen through the years, Reverend Shanks studied for a moment. "Besides the changes in technology, there have been so many, many changes in the people themselves— the way they live—the way they conduct themselves, both in the community and in the Church. It used to be that our communi- ties—and our churches—were stable. People were born there, they lived there and they died there. It wasn't unusual for me to baptize someone when they were a child, marry that person when they got grown, and preach their funeral when they died. Now, people move in and out all the time. It's harder to know your neighbors and the people around you. That makes it harder to trust people—because you don't know them. That's just the way it is."

As Reverend Shanks reflected on his long and distinguished ca- reer, he speculated about the future. "I'm not done, yet" he says, with a great deal of conviction. "I expect to see a lot more changes before I go on in. The Lord promised me 'way more than 100 years'—and I'm not there yet. As long as I have my health and still feel good, I intend to keep on preaching."

"The Lord's not done with me yet!!!"

Author's note: In July 2005, Rev. Shanks celebrated his 100th birthday . . . and is still preaching.

Zion Watchtower Baptist Church

FORT BEND COUNTY

"I'll help out—temporary—till you can get somebody else."

In 1891, the Zion Watchtower Baptist Church was organized, northeast of Richmond, on what is now FM 359, as a branch of the First Mt. Carmel Baptist Church in Richmond. It was organized by Rev. G. W. Smith.

The first pastor was Rev. Elijah Crooms. The first deacons were Juis Sherman, Tom Sherman, Steve Wilson, Jeff Smith, Davis McDonald, and Henry Howard.

In those early years, services were held under a brush arbor. It was not until 1920 that the first building was erected. That structure was destroyed by a storm in 1932. A new building went up in 1934. Rev R. E. Edwards pastored the church during these years.

Rev. B. J. Shanks

In 1948, Rev. J. B. Gaslin was elected as pastor. In 1953, as Rev. Gaslin's health began to fail, Rev. B. J. Shanks filled in for him—on a temporary basis. In 1956, Rev. Gaslin died, and Rev. Shanks was elected as pastor. He has served as pastor ever since—for forty-seven years.

The church building was re-modeled in the 1960s and served until 2000, when the need for a larger and more modern facility led to the construction of a new church building. The new build-

106

Zion Watchtower Baptist Church—old

ing was finished in December, 2000, and was dedicated in January, 2001.

The Zion Watchtower Church is a strong and stable church today—with a solid membership. It continues to function—and serve—under the leadership of Rev. Shanks, now ninety-seven. As Rev. Shanks puts it "The Lord's not done with me yet."

Zion Watchtower Baptist Church—new

Greater Oak Grove Baptist Church
Leon County

"This has been our church for over eighty years."

"I'm ninety-two now. I joined the Greater Oak Grove Church when I was nine years old. I've been a member ever since" Mrs. Smith reminisced. "My husband, David, is ninety-three, and he joined about the same time I did.

"Rev. Reese Whitfield was the pastor when I joined in 1919. Ed Middleton and Johnny Logan are the only two old deacons I can remember. Ed Middleton gave the land for the church."

"The church used to be across the road from where it is now" adds Mr. Smith. "They taught school in the church building back then. I can't remember all the old preachers, but I remember Rev. Perkins and Rev. Sutton."

Mr. and Mrs. Dave Smith.

Greater Oak Grove Baptist Church.

There apparently is little written record of the history of the church, located southeast of Centerville, on CR 122, in the Egypt Community. The cornerstone on the church indicates the church was established in 1872 and the present building was erected in 1948. The pastor was B. C. Dixion, and deacons were H. J. Middleton, F. Wiley, A. Pickett, and H. D. Davis.

"We're probably the two oldest members of the church. We still attend the services whenever we can. We have services once a month, on the third Sunday, and we have pretty good crowds" says Mrs. Smith. "We have a homecoming once a year, in August, and lots of folks that grew up here come back for that. Rev. Algie Robinson is our pastor now."

"This has been our church for over eighty years" adds Mr. Smith. "It has always meant a lot to us. It will still be our church for as long as we live."

Mossy Grove Methodist Church

LAVACA COUNTY

"Hurricane Carla destroyed it . . . but they rebuilt it."

September 30, 1962 was a big day for the members of the Mossy Grove Methodist Church, located on CR 1, about six miles south of Hallettsville. This was the day their new building was dedicated.

The old building had been heavily damaged the year before by Hurricane Carla . . . and, for a time, it was uncertain whether or not the church would be rebuilt. The membership was small at that time . . . but, as a result of a lot of hard work—and with the help of the Hallettsville Methodist Church—money was raised, and the church was rebuilt.

The Mossy Grove Church has a long and rich history. According to Paul Boethel's "History of Lavaca County," the Mossy Grove Church was organized in 1855, by Rev. John Cook. The charter members were Berryman Hall and his wife and daugh-

Mossy Grove Methodist Church.

110

ter, John Livergood and wife, Miss Lucretia Woodward, Mrs. Lucinda Woodward, John Nolen and wife, A. G. Nolen, John Long and Sarah Long.

Except for the period during the Civil War (when services were held only on an irregular and sporadic basis) the Mossy Grove Church has functioned continuously ever since.

No records exist prior to 1872, but at that time, records showed a membership of about 150. This was the only rural Methodist church in Lavaca County to survive the economic readjustments of the late 1800s, and as late as 1914 reported seventy-three members.

The Mossy Grove Methodist Church continues to function today, under the leadership of Rev. Lundy Hooten, with services two Sundays per month. It has served the needs of its members— and of the community—for almost 150 years and is expecting to do so for a long time to come.

Mt. Vernon Baptist Church

HOUSTON COUNTY

"The center of the community life."

"I'm seventy-seven years old and I've been going to church here at Mt. Vernon all my life . . . I've actually been a member for about sixty years now," recounts John Earl Dowdy. "My daddy attended church here before me . . . along with my uncles, aunts and cousins. The church has just always been a part of my life . . . for as long as I can remember."

Located northeast of Ratcliff, on CR 1155, the Mt. Vernon Baptist Church is believed to have been formed about 1871—the first grave in the Mt. Vernon Cemetery is dated in 1872. The site was probably picked because of the strong spring located nearby. It was used as a community wash place and eventually sort of evolved

Mt. Vernon Baptist Church

112

into a central meeting place. The first building was just a rough un-
finished structure and was used as both a church and a school. It
was used by both Baptists and Methodists in those early days. The
building burned about 1883. A new building was erected a year later
and it was given a name—for the first time—Mt. Vernon. It continued to function as a union church for several years—until a
Methodist church was organized nearby at Old Ratcliff. In April,
1888, the Mt. Vernon Baptist Church was formally organized and
has functioned continuously ever since.

"In 1960, we tore down the old building and built a new one,
using a lot of the lumber from the old building" says Mr. Dowdy,
who is a Senior Deacon.

"The church has always been very, very important to us" he
says. "It holds our community together. It has always reacted to the
needs of the community. Whenever a tragedy happens in the community, the people always come together to deal with it and to help
out." Mrs. Dowdy, who did not grow up here, but has been a member for many years, echoes those sentiments.

"Our membership is small now—on a typical Sunday we usually
have about twenty to forty folks attending services—but our membership is pretty stable. We have a few young people in our church.
We have services every Sunday . . . Rev. Gerald Hollis is our pastor.
We plan on being here for a long, long time yet."

Social Grove Missionary Baptist Church

LEON COUNTY

"Gone . . . but not forgotten."

The Social Grove Missionary Baptist Church, located between Centerville and Buffalo, on CR 278, is believed to have been organized in 1905. That's when land was deeded for a church and cemetery. It was a "split-off" from the nearby Siloam Baptist Church. Other than that, there is little formal record of the history of the church.

Some years ago, Mrs. Barney Watson, who lived nearby virtually all her life, wrote down what she knew of the history of the church (it was published in *The History of Leon County*). According to Mrs. Watson, some of the early pastors were Rev. C. G. Stevens, Rev. Hurt, and Rev. James. Another preacher, Rev. Paul Bearfield,

Social Grove Baptist Church.

114

conducted several revivals at the church. Mrs. Watson's husband, Barney Watson, served as Sunday School Superintendent for many years.

Although it apparently was never a very large church (there are only twelve graves in the adjacent cemetery), the Social Grove Church functioned steadily, for many years, as a strong, stable church, and as a vital and important part of the community.

With the decline in rural populations after World War II, the church began to suffer, and apparently held services somewhat sporadically during the late 1940s and 1950s—probably whenever they could get a preacher there. Finally, sometime in the early 1960s, they just didn't have enough people left—and the church closed for good.

The old building is still there—just barely—along with the tiny little cemetery. There are no doors on the building and it probably won't remain upright much longer, but—for a while, at least—it's still there, serving as a silent reminder of "What used to be—in days gone by."

Wheeler Springs Baptist Church

HOUSTON COUNTY

"Like a rock."

The Wheeler Springs Baptist Church, located on CR 2106, west of Crockett, had its beginning in 1885, as a community church. A few families (Taylor, Warfield, Richardson, Demby, Hunter, Murphy, Lewis, Mitchell, and Shepherd) erected a crude building, so they would have a place to worship. The following year, 1886, Bro. Ned King and wife, Nettie, along with Bro. and Mrs. Sime Stell, started a prayer service and a Sunday School (It wasn't until 1910 that they got their first Sunday School books).

The third Sunday of each month was set aside for preaching services. They welcomed any traveling preacher they could get. Rev. Mango Lane was one of the first preachers to preach here.

Mrs. Wesley Taylor Fobbs has done extensive research on the

Mrs. Wesley Taylor Fobbs

history of the church. Over the years, Mrs. Fobbs has served the Wheeler Springs Church in numerous capacities—Sunday School teacher, mission teacher, bible teacher, program committee, Sunday School superintendent, and assistant Secretary. According to Mrs. Fobbs, in 1928, it was decided that a better building was needed. French Taylor donated land and Ed Murphy led the effort to build a new church. Murphy, along with Monroe Hunter, Sidney King and Rev. Harr Mitchell, bought the lumber and hauled it to the site in wagons. All the members

116

Wheeler Springs Baptist Church.

joined in to construct the building. In the same year, Rev. Andrew Moore formally organized a church—and the Wheeler Springs Baptist Church was officially born. The first deacons were Monroe Hunter, Sidney King and Ed Murphy. Records indicate the first pastor, Rev. Moore, was paid $25 per month.

In 1944, the pastor at that time, Rev. J. T. Groves (he was the 4th pastor) decided the church needed a better and bigger building. At this time—during World War II—lumber was hard to get . . . so they decided to build a rock building. The members gathered rocks wherever they could get them and hauled them to the site in wagons. With the assistance of William Lacy, a rock mason from Palestine, the very unique building was constructed . . . and is still in use today.

Throughout the years, the church has had only nine pastors— Rev. Moore, Rev. W. H. Dixon, Rev. J. L. Ward, Rev. J. T. Groves, Rev. J. C. Nicholas, Rev. C. W. Wilson, Rev. J. Reed, Rev. J. Aldridge, and Rev. Dennis Gainers, who continues to lead the church today. The membership is small today, but they still have services once a month—on the third Sunday—and they have Sunday School on a more regular basis.

"I've been a member of Wheeler Springs Baptist Church for about seventy years" says Mrs. Fobbs. "I joined the church when I was about thirteen years old, and I've been a member ever since. My whole family—my parents and all my brothers and sisters—we all sort of grew up in this church. It was always a very, very important part of our lives. For me, it still is . . . and it always will be."

Two-Mile Methodist Church

LEON COUNTY

"Two miles from where???"

It sits there, on the banks of Two Mile Creek, on FM 977, about five miles east of Leona, where it has been for many, many years, serving the needs of its members, and of the Two Mile Community.

According to information put together by Ms. Rhonda Kizzee, Mrs. Melissia Kizzee, Mrs. Lemma Mae Hopkins Silas, and Ms. Lula V. Johnson, the church was first organized in 1865, by a group of former slaves, and the first building was a small one room log cabin, with a dirt floor. It was located on the Holley property, not too far away from the present location. It is believed the original

Two Mile Methodist Church

founders were Jesse Hopkins, Rufus Davis, Louis Holley, Jake Washington, Wash McDaniel, Dady Davis, Charles McDaniel, Austin Townsend, Henry King, King Davis, Richard Washington, Frank Moten, Houston Davis, Andy Harrison, and Billy Washington. It was called "First Church" at that time, and the first pastor was Rev. Andy Harrison. Later, they worshipped under a brush arbor, on the nearby Prince property. A few years later, under the leadership of Rev. Frank Moten, the church was relocated to a spot behind the present location.

Sometime in the early 1900s, the name was changed to Two Mile Methodist Episcopal Church. The "Two Mile" name reflects its proximity to the Two Mile Creek—and the Two Mile Community. However, no one seems to know anything about the origin of the "Two Mile" name. Is it two miles from some particular spot? If so, where? Apparently, nothing exists to answer that question. On the cornerstone of the church, the name is spelled "Tu Mile." No one appears to know if there is any significance to this discrepancy.

In 1924, a new church was constructed. That building was later replaced by the present structure.

In 1925, the church bought its first piano . . . and thus began a musical tradition that continues right up through the present time. The Two Mile Church has long been known for its great music, throughout the years. There have been many singing groups (most of them family groups) that have performed here—and gained recognition—not just within the Two Mile Community, but throughout surrounding areas as well. The James Polk family, J. L. King, Garfield Reed, and Sammy Davis have been among the better known performers. Other area singers often perform at Two Mile . . . among them Jack Jones, the George Reed family, and others.

As was the case with many rural churches, all-day singing programs were commonly held at the church. Usually held on a Sunday afternoon, these programs would attract not only the local members, but visitors from all around the surrounding area—and sometimes from Houston, Dallas and other "far away" places. Normal services usually would be held in the morning, and then, about noon when the preaching services were concluded, there would be "dinner on the ground." Everyone knew to bring food, and it was all put on the tables under the oak trees, and shared by all. After the meal was over, the music began. It was usually a very informal program. Anyone who wanted to perform was free to do so. This type of program was where many singers (and groups) got their start.

The Two Mile Church has had many pastors through the years. In 1933, a new pastor, Rev. L. S. Lamb, came to the church. He was widower with eight children. It is said that during his tenure, the entire community pitched in, on a regular basis, to help raise and care for his children.

"My father, Rev. V. E. Johnson, became the pastor of the Two Mile Church in 1966" recalls Ms. Lula Johnson. "He remained as pastor until he died, in 1981." This is an unusually long tenure for a Methodist preacher.

The Two Mile Methodist Church , under the leadership of Rev. Carey Cauley, Jr., still functions today, still maintains its tradition of great music, and still strives to meet the spiritual needs of its members, and of the Two Mile community. It appears it will continue to do so for a long time to come. Who knows? . . . perhaps someday, we will even find out where it is two miles from.

Rev. and Mrs. V. E. Johnson
—Courtesy of Ms. Lula Johnson

Wilderness Branch Baptist Church

FORT BEND COUNTY

"He served as pastor for sixty years."

There is little written record of the early history of the Wilderness Branch Baptist Church. It is believed that the church was begun about 1900 as a branch of the nearby Spring Green Baptist Church.

According to Mrs. Middie Cobbin, a lifelong member of the church, Rev. Jake Sanders—a member of the Spring Green Church—was assigned the responsibility of organizing the new church and serving as its new pastor. It is believed this was his first charge.

Wilderness Branch Baptist Church

Apparently, Rev. Sanders held services originally under a brush arbor. In 1904, Mary Briscoe deeded one acre of land to the church. It is assumed the building was erected shortly thereafter—probably by the members themselves.

Rev. Sanders must have felt very comfortable with his duties and responsibilities here . . . he remained as pastor of the Wilderness Branch Church for sixty years.

The Wilderness Branch Church, located on FM 359, north of Richmond-Rosenberg, still functions today, under the leadership of Rev. W. T. Moses. Although the membership is small, they still have services on a regular schedule, every Sunday. According to Mrs. Cobbin, their membership is fairly stable.

With new subdivisions springing up all around it—and a brand new huge school complex almost next door, the Wilderness Branch Baptist Church, in its majestic appearance, serves as a reminder of "the way things used to be."

Union Baptist Church of Ten Mile

MADISON COUNTY

"Ten Miles from where???"

In 1887, a group of citizens in the Ten Mile Community, located between Madisonville and Normangee . . . about ten miles from Madisonville . . . gathered together and formed a church. Located on what is now FM 2289, they named it the Union Baptist Church of Ten Mile.

The first pastor was A. A. Allen and the first deacons were Levi Harper, A. J. Bledsoe, A. M. Hill, and M. Risinger. Some of the early families were the Bledsoe, Batson, Cobb, Harper, Risinger, Rigby, Ethridge, Farrar, Gustavus, and Farrar families

According to Jerry Gustavus, a life-long member of the Union Baptist Church "We've had three different buildings, over the years. The first building was on the same side of the road as the present

Union Baptist Church of Ten Mile.

123

building—adjacent to the Ten Mile Cemetery. Then, from about 1940 till 1955, they used what had been the Ten Mile School building, located on the opposite side of the road. Then, in 1955, FM 2289 was built, and it was felt the church needed to be on the same side of the road as the cemetery. So, they tore down the old school building and used the lumber to build the present building. We moved in the new building in January, 1956."

As with most old country churches, the Ten Mile Church was a vital part of the community. Says Mr. Gustavus "I grew up in the Ten Mile Church. It's just always been there for us. There was a time when we struggled . . . but now, we're a strong, stable church. We've been growing over the past three or four years. We have a good many young folks in the church and we usually have about forty folks in Sunday School and about fifty to sixty for preaching."

"Rev. Vernon Powell is our pastor now and we have services every Sunday. We're going to be here for a long, long time yet."

A Call From Who???

"What he heard was Rody Keeling's old Jackass a-braying!!"

When I was growing up on a farm in East Texas (Leon County), in the 1940s, things were different from today. We didn't own an alarm clock—we had no need for one. My daddy kept a Jackass, for stud purposes—and that Jackass served as our alarm clock. Most of our farm work was done then by mules . . . thus there was a great demand for mules. (For the benefit of the uninformed, a mule is a hybrid—and sterile—cross between a horse and a jackass.) Our jackass was the only one in the community, and due to his unusually loud "voice" he was well known throughout the community. On a still day, he could be heard welcoming the new day with his braying (always at daybreak) for a good three or four miles. It could be said that he served the entire community as he delivered his "wake up call."

About a mile up the road from our house was the Evans Chapel

Charlie Wood Lamb
—Courtesy of Dorothy Hitt

Methodist Church. This was the only church in the community, and it served as the center of the community life. The Evans Chapel Church had a unique claim to fame. It claimed (probably correctly) to have sent more of its members (on a percentage basis) on to the ministry than any other Methodist church in the state.

Thus, it was not a particularly unusual event when it was announced that one of the teenage members, Charlie Wood Lamb, had "heard the call" and was going to become a preacher. Charlie was the oldest of the Lamb boys. The Lamb family members were regulars in church every Sunday. Charlie's daddy (my great-uncle) taught the adult Sunday School class for some thirty years. The Lamb family always sat in the right-hand section, second pew from the front. That was their pew . . . no one else was allowed to sit there. This was not an uncommon custom in small rural churches.

Garnet House, et al.

—Courtesy of Dorothy Hitt

Charlie's lifestyle, at that point, had been pretty much typical of that of his peers. While he had never been in any serious trouble, he had not exactly led a life of angelic innocence. He had been known to swipe a watermelon or two. He and his best friend and cousin, Garnet House (Author's note . . . Garnet House was my uncle) had once gotten in trouble for illegally "telephoning" catfish in Boggy Creek. Charlie and Uncle Garnet once burned down an old abandoned cotton gin because they overheard Grandpa House complain about what an eye-sore the old gin was, and how he wished lightning would strike it and burn it down. Charlie and Uncle Garnet had, more than once, tipped over an out-house, without any particular regard to whether or not it might be occupied.

My Great-Aunt Ida Shepherd, then well up in age, was known for her cynicism and skepticism and was never reluctant to express those traits in very blunt and caustic terms. Aunt Ida was a small woman, was somewhat stooped and walked with a cane. She always wore high necked, long sleeved, ankle length dresses in some shade of black or gray. She was never shy about offering her opinions about most anything. In today's terminology, Aunt Ida would probably be described as a "tough sell."

When told of Charlie's "calling," she expressed her doubts very bluntly. She tapped her cane of the floor for emphasis, "I've known that Lamb boy all his life" she snorted, "And I can tell you for sure, that boy didn't get no call from the Lord! What he heard was Rody Keeling's old jackass a-braying!!!"

Aunt Ida may have been right; At that point in his life, Charlie had never been noted for his attention to detail. At any rate, Charlie heard the "call" (regardless of its source). He answered that call, responding to it appro-

George and Ida Shepherd
—Family photo

priately. He made appropriate changes in his lifestyle and devoted his life to the ministry. He went on to a long and distinguished career as a Methodist minister.

In addition, Charlie's two younger half-brothers, Lee and Clifton, later became Methodist ministers, as well. Another brother, James, became a minister of another denomination. Ironically, Uncle Garnet later became a Methodist minister himself, as did his younger brother, Morris. Later, Uncle Garnet's two sons, Jerry and Jimmy House, became Methodist ministers, as did his grandson, Jerry, Jr. Had she lived long enough, Aunt Ida would have been surprised.

I'm not sure there is a moral to this story. However, if there is one, it might be simply this: "Never ignore what you may hear, regardless of its source. It might turn out to be something important and worthwhile . . . even if it comes straight out of the mouth of a genuine jackass."

New South Salem Baptist Church

LEON COUNTY

"We started with a Rev. Robinson . . . and now, we're back to a Rev. Robinson."

In June, 1865, when the news of Emancipation finally reached Texas, the suddenly freed slaves were at a loss as to what to do and how to adjust to their new status and conditions. Many of them began to wander aimlessly from place to place. A large group went north and settled in Kansas for awhile. They weren't satisfied there and, in the summer of 1866, they returned to Texas.

Some of the wanderers settled in Leon County, between Centerville and Jewett, in a community they named Salem. They needed a permanent place to worship. According to Mrs. Louise Perkins, a long-time resident of the community, these few families,

New South Salem Baptist Church

129

with the help of a White preacher named Clayborn, organized and built what may have been the first Black church built in Leon County. They named it the New South Salem Baptist Church. It is believed the first pastor was Rev. Cain Robinson. Research done by Mrs. Perkins indicates that other early pastors included: Rev. John Perkins, Rev. Sharce Haines, Rev. Prescott, Rev. John Carson, Rev. S. V. Herbert, Rev. Thomas, Rev. W. R. Estill, Rev. Thomas Lee, and Rev. J. A. Jenkins. Some of the original families included the Robinson, Henderson, Broncson, Reed, and Haynes families.

Eventually, a disagreement arose among the congregation, and some of the members left the church, moved across the creek, and formed the North Salem Church. Later, they reconciled, and once again, there was only the South Salem Church. The church remained at the original location until 1956, when it was relocated at the present site, on CR 322.

Although the membership is small now, the church still meets regularly, on the first Sunday of the month. The present pastor is Rev. Algie Robinson, a great-grandson of Rev. Cain Robinson, the first pastor. Mrs. Perkins, who has been a member of the church for 50 years, serves as Secretary, Treasurer, and Acting Superintendent of the Sunday School. As Mrs. Perkins puts it, "We're hanging on. The church is still very important to us. It means a lot to us—and to the community. We started with a Robinson . . . and now, we're back to a Robinson. We hope we will still be going for a long time, yet . . . and we hope Rev. Robinson will still be here to lead us."

Pilgrim Predestination Regular Baptist Church

ANDERSON COUNTY

"A church that was truly on the move."

Located southwest of Elkhart, the Pilgrim Predestination Regular Baptist Church is generally recognized as the first Protestant church in Texas. How it achieved that position, however, makes for a very unusual story.

In 1832, Elder Daniel Parker, living in Illinois at the time, felt a need to move to Texas to establish a church. On his exploratory trip to Texas, however, he discovered that there would be some problems. This was prior to Texas independence (Actually, there was no Texas at that time—it was a part of Mexico). The Catholic Church was the official church of Mexico, and Mexican law forbade the establishment of any church, other than Catholic, in Texas. It

Pilgrim Predestination Baptist Church

appeared, however, that any churches already established would be allowed to continue to function.

Elder Parker had a brainstorm. He returned to Illinois, and on July 26, 1833, he organized the Pilgrim Predestination Regular Baptist Church—and began the long, arduous task of moving it to Texas.

We don't know how many people were involved, but there were twenty-five wagons in the caravan. They stopped in Claiborne Parish, Louisiana, on October 20, 1833, and held a church service. They stopped again on January 12, 1834, near what is now the town of Anderson, Texas and had another service. They eventually settled down near Fort Brown, on San Pedro Creek, in what is now Houston County—holding services wherever they could, usually in the homes of members.

It was from here that some of the members of the Parker family moved to what is now the Groesbeck area and established the ill-fated Fort Parker. On May 19, 1836, in that infamous Indian raid on Fort Parker, John Parker, Isaac Parker, and Ben Parker were killed and Cynthia Ann Parker was captured. James W. Parker survived and returned to Fort Houston, near the present site of Palestine. All the surviving Parker's then relocated back to the Anderson/Houston County area.

They eventually built a permanent church—a simple log building with a dirt floor. In 1859, it was replaced with a box-like build-

Reproduction of original church.

Interior of original church.

ing, and in 1890, it, in turn, was replaced with a larger frame building. In 1929, a brick building was erected—that building still stands today. An exact replica of the original log building has been constructed and sits there, next to the brick structure.

The church now is used only for special occasions. In the adjacent cemetery rest six generations of Elder Daniel Parker's family. It is unlikely the church will ever move from its present location ... but it sure moved—a long ways—at one time.

(Note: Much of the information contained herein was taken from a November 28, 1948 article in the Houston Chronicle magazine.)

Camp Zion-Rising Star United Baptist Church

WHARTON COUNTY

"Together again . . . after 114 years."

In 1870, Rev. Hillary Hooks, a former slave, organized the Camp Zion Baptist Church, in the Spanish Camp Community, north of Wharton. Some of the early families were Anderson, Coleman, Hatton, Hill, Jefferson, Ray, Runnel, Skane, Wygal, Bryant, Davis, Hawkins, Hooks, Moses, Robertson, Sanders, and Walker. Rev. Hooks served as pastor until 1884, when Rev. R. B. Evans assumed the position.

It is not known whether or not they had a permanent building in those early years, but, in 1887, James Winston gave land, along what is now FM 1161, and sometime after that (it is not known exactly when) a building was erected.

Old Camp Zion Baptist Church

Old Rising Star Baptist Church.

In 1888, a division occurred within the church—the reasons for the division have long since been lost—and a part of the membership left and organized a new church (called the Rising Star Baptist Church) not far away, on what is now the Glen Flora Road. Later—it is not known exactly when—the church was moved to its present location, on what is now FM 640. It is believed that Rev. R. P. Kaiser organized the Rising Star Baptist Church. The founding families were Jones, Taylor, Robertson, Hawkins, Gordon, Shanes and Walker (for many years, Sister Priscilla Walker was known as the "Mother of the Church").

For more than 100 years, these two churches continued to function, located less than two miles apart.

"I grew up in the Spanish Camp Community," relates Rev. Clarence Owens, "and I attended the Camp Zion Church when I was a child." Rev. Owens later joined the army and moved away—staying away for some forty years.

"After I left the military, I went to Alvin, working in construction. I started preaching in 1974, but I still worked full time. Later I worked for Amoco. In 1995, I retired (I was working in Louisiana at the time) and I moved back "home"—to Spanish Camp.

Rev. Owens joined the Rising Star church, and then, not long after—in 1996—a pastoral vacancy occurred at the Camp Zion church. Rev. Owens was called to fill that vacancy, and he accepted the call.

Rev. Clarence Owens

"The congregation at Camp Zion was small—we only had about three families—but we had services every other Sunday" recalls Rev. Owens. "Then, in 1997, the pastor at Rising Star died, and I was called to that position. I accepted, and pastored both churches, conducting services at the two churches on alternate Sundays.

"Almost immediately, I started thinking about the possibility of consolidating the two churches. It just didn't make sense to continue with these two churches, only a mile and a half apart, with small congregations, when all these folks at the two churches knew one another. In fact, most of them were kin to one another and none of them even knew what caused the original split—some 110 years earlier. The reasons for that split had long been lost and forgotten.

"In 1998, we made the proposal for consolidation . . . and actually, there was very little opposition to it—it just made good sense. In January 1999, we closed the Camp Zion building . . . it was getting in pretty bad shape . . . and started having all the services at Rising Star, but we still maintained the two separate congregational memberships. We started making plans for a new sanctuary, in between the two locations. It took two years to get it done. We moved into the new church building in April 2002."

New Camp Zion–Rising Star Baptist Church

Located near the intersection of FM 640 and 1161, the new building houses what is now called the Camp Zion–Rising Star United Baptist Church.

As Rev. Owens puts it "After 114 years, we're back together again . . . I think it was just meant to be."

/\t. Zion Baptist Church

LEON COUNTY

"There's a lot still to be done."

The Mt. Zion Baptist Church, located about one mile west of Leona, just off FM 977, was formed in 1895. It is believed the church was organized by Rev. Tony Hubert, Rev. Gus Harraway, Rev. Jerry Rhinehart, and Rev. Cain Robinson.

According to Mrs. Katherine Polk, the church Secretary, the land for the church was donated by Billy Rogers. It is believed the first pastor was Rev. Gus Harraway. The original building is still in use—with some additions that were added later.

Some of the early deacons were Allen Jones, Mark Perkins, Henry Dotson, Jake Simpson, James Evans, Arch Proctor, Luther

Mt. Zion Baptist Church

Allen, Jake Brown, H. Norris, General Green, J. E. Starkey, Connie Perkins, Charley Taylor, T. D. Drewey, Roy Dawkins, and Jack Brooks. Ray Dawkins, and Jack Jones are currently serving as Deacons. Jack Jones, incidentally, is a renowned gospel singer, and performs regularly throughout the entire area.

Over the years, the Mt. Zion Church has produced four ministers from its ranks—Rev. S. M. Jones, Rev. Joe Branch, Rev. Jake Brown and Rev. Louis Thompson.

Although its numbers are down, the Mt. Zion Church still has services two Sundays per month, under its present pastor, Rev. Bobby Madkins.

Jack Jones

"We're down now to about eight to ten regular members" says Mrs. Polk. "So many of the older ones have gone on in . . . and there's just not many young ones coming on to take their place. But the Mt. Zion Church was built on 'Faith and Works' . . . and there's a lot yet to be done. To those of us that are left, the Mt. Zion Church is still our church. It's still very, very important to us . . . just like it always has been . . . and just like it always will be."

/\t. Pleasant CME Church

HOUSTON COUNTY

"We just don't have many folks left any more."

"I grew up in the Mt. Pleasant CME Church . . . I joined when I was about eleven or twelve years old, and I'm seventy-one now" recounts Mrs. Clemons David. "That church has always been a very, very important part of the lives of the people in the community."

According to the best information available, the church was organized around 1885, with Rev. Peter Steward as the first pastor. Although formal records are lacking, it is believed that among the early families were the O'Neil, Berry and Quantril families.

Located on CR 4200, west of Pennington, the original building was replaced by a second structure in 1900. That building served

Mt. Pleasant CME Church

until it was destroyed by a tornado in 1941. The present building replaced that one.

For many years, the church was the center of the community life. Then, as population patterns changed, membership began to drop.

"We just don't have many folks left any more" says Mrs. David. "We had to stop having regular services in 1999 . . . we just didn't have enough people. We use the church once in awhile for special occasions now, and we have a Homecoming every year on the 3rd Sunday in August.

"But no matter what happens, the Mt. Pleasant Church will always be there—in our hearts."

New Pleasant Hill Baptist Church

HOUSTON COUNTY

"Church ranked right up there with school and parents."

The New Pleasant Hill Baptist Church is located on CR 1650, southeast of Grapeland, in the Germany Community. And yes—it is located on a hill—a very pleasant hill.

The early history of the church is somewhat vague, but it is believed the church probably was organized sometime around 1870. The land was donated by John and Jane Burt. The original building was located across the road from the present site and was used as a school as well. Early families were Moore, Duren, Allen, Hall, Berryman and Bell.

It is not known, for sure, when the present building was constructed, but according to Mrs. Florarean Overshown, the church

New Pleasant Hill Baptist Church

142

secretary, "I'm seventy-eight years old and I can remember, as a small child, seeing it built—so it's probably about seventy years old. I grew up in this church . . . I joined when I was twelve years old. This church was a very, very important part of our lives. Everybody knew everybody else . . . in fact, most of us were related to one another. The kids respected the grown-ups. We looked up to them and they helped guide us along the right path, as we grew up. The church ranked right up there with the school and our parents as the most important factor in our lives."

Mrs. Overshown moved away when she was in her twenties but always maintained her contacts with the church. "This church was still 'home' even when I was living in Houston" she says. When she retired, sixteen years ago, she moved back "I came back home—to my community and to my church."

The New Pleasant Hill Baptist Church still sits there . . . on that same hill, still serving the community, under the leadership of Rev. Joe L. Ard (he has pastored the church since 1972). Like so many of the country churches, the numbers are small today.

"So many of the older folks have passed on . . . and the younger ones have moved away. But for those of us that are still here, this is still our church. We still have services twice a month" says Mrs. Overshown. "No matter what happens, this will always be our church."

Middle Branch Missionary Baptist Church

LEON COUNTY

"All of my children were baptized here."

There apparently is very little written documentation of the early days of the Middle Branch Missionary Baptist Church, located on CR 404, between Leona and Normangee. It is believed the church was established in 1910 . . . and at one time there was a

Mrs. Moidree Walker and Mrs. Mable Young, cooking stew for a church function.
—Courtesy of Mrs. Walker

school there, as well. The church is probably named for a small creek—or branch—that is located right across the road.

About a year ago, the oldest member of the church, Mrs. Mable Young, died at ninety-one . . . and a lot of the history of the church probably disappeared with her. Mrs. Moidree Walker, eighty-four, is one of the older remaining members. "I've been a member since about 1935," she says. "All of my children were baptized here and were members till they grew up and moved away. This church has been a big part of my life for as long as I can remember."

It is not known who the first pastor was, but, according to Mrs. Walker, some of the early families included the Washington, Williams, Robinson, Goodwyn, Tryon, Madkins, and Leyman families. Frank Williams served as a deacon for over forty years. Robert Madkins, at various times, served the church as Sunday School

Middle Branch Baptist Church

Left: *Rev.
Robert
Madkins.
Photo from
funeral notice.*
—Courtesy of
Mrs. Walker

Right: *Mrs.
Moidree
Walker*

teacher, Sunday School superintendent, deacon and pastor . . . in fact, he probably pastored the church longer than any other preacher. The present pastor is Bobby Madkins, a son of Robert Madkins.

"Our membership is small now . . . we don't have many young folks left any more" says Mrs. Walker. "We have services one Sunday a month . . . and, once a year, we have a big Homecoming celebration. Even though there's not many of us left any more, the church is still very, very important to all of us that are left . . . it always will be."

Piney Creek Missionary Baptist Church

HOUSTON COUNTY

"It rose from the dead . . . and was resurrected."

According to information furnished by Mrs. Erma Currie, the Piney Creek Missionary Baptist Church, located seven miles south of Kennard, on FM 2781, was originally organized in 1891, with eleven charter members: C. T. Page, Mrs. Sarah Page, J. M. Stubblefield, Anginila Stubblefield, Mrs. Dennis Key, J. M. Baker, Z. P. Stewart, Richard Butler, J. M. Carlton, E. J. Carlton, and Mrs. James Best. The first pastor was Rev. J. M. Carlton. They had no building at this time and they met and worshipped under a brush arbor about four miles south of Kennard.

Piney Creek Baptist Church.

146

After a period of time—we're not sure exactly when—the church became inactive.

On August 31, 1915, C. T. Page, Della Stubblefield, Alva Page Baker, Cara Page, T. A. Stubblefield, Lillie Page, S. A. Morgan, and Mattie Morgan met south of Kennard to reorganize and reactivate the church. Rev. C. M. Carlton was, once again, selected as pastor. The deacons elected were C. T. Page and J. R. Stubblefield.

There is no indication of whether the church had a building at this time. We do know that in 1929, under the leadership of Rev. J. R. Foster, the church moved to its present location and erected a new building. That structure is still in use today.

The Piney Creek Missionary Baptist Church continues to function today, holding services on a regular schedule. Rev. Michael Moore is the present pastor.

Pleasant Grove CME Church

HOUSTON COUNTY

"So many have gone on in."

"I don't know for sure when the church organized, but it was sometime in the late 1800's. We know that in 1894, Henry Campbell and his wife gave one acre of land for the church. I've been a member for seventy-six years—I'm eighty-eight now and I joined when I was twelve years old," Port Arthur Todd relates what he knows of the history of the Pleasant Grove CME, located west of Crockett at 2076 Halls Bluff Road.

"Some of the first families were Todd, Washington, Boozeman, Wagner, Owens, Gardner, Delaney, Houston, Merrick and Blake.

Port Arthur Todd

You can still find members of these same families here in the community. The first pastor was a Rev. Jones. The first building was a log house—they also used it for a school. Originally the CME name stood for Colored Methodist Episcopal. In 1957, that was changed to Christian Methodist Episcopal.

"In the old days, the church was the center of our community. We had lots of social events, as well as religious events at the church... singing programs, prayer meetings, revivals, and all kinds of special events.

148

Pleasant Grove CME Church.

"On February 27, 1995, our church burned. We rebuilt. We're small now . . . so many of the young ones have moved away and so many of the older ones have gone on in . . . but we're still hanging on. We have services once a month—our pastor is Rev. Kervin Kinz—and our church is still very, very important to us—just like it has always been. We don't intend to give it up."

Simpson Chapel Missionary Baptist Church

HOUSTON COUNTY

"If I'm not the oldest member, I'm sure right up there close to the top."

"I wasn't an original member of the church, but I joined in 1944," says Joe Garrett. "I grew up in Cherokee County, around Alto, and we moved here in 1931. I'm ninety years old now . . . if I'm not the oldest member, I'm sure right up there close to the top of the list."

"As far as I know, there's not any written record of the history of the church . . . but I was always told it was organized in 1939, and a Rev. Hall was the first pastor. Rev. Hezikiah Morrison was the second pastor. The church was originally across the road from where it is now. This is the third building. It was built sometime in the 1950s, under Rev. Simmons.

"Some of the early families—best as I can remember—were Brown, Washington, Simpson, Wylie, Chatman and Scott."

Joe Garrett

Harry Scott, a Deacon, has been a member for sixty-two years. "I joined when I was ten years old" he says. "At that time it was known as the Whitely Baptist Church, located about a half mile from FM 227. Sometime around 1943, a division took place in the church, and some of the members left and formed the Simpson Chapel Church. The old Whitely Church has been gone for a long time now.

"Rev. Detroit Woolbright was our

pastor for twenty-eight years, till his health got bad and he had to resign."

Located on FM 227, northwest of Ratcliff, the Simpson Chapel Church, under the leadership of Rev. Lionel Whitaker, the present pastor, is today a strong, stable church.

"In fact, we're growing" says Mr. Garrett. "We've got lots of young folks in the church and we've got a real active membership.

"I've been a deacon for over forty years now and I've been a senior Sunday School teacher for a long time. I don't get around too good now—so I don't make it to church every Sunday, but I go as often as I can. This church has always been very important to me . . . and it always will be."

Harry Scott.

Simpson Chapel Baptist Church.

Zion Lutheran Church of Sublime

LAVACA COUNTY

"They tore it down and moved it to Sublime."

Sometime in the early 1850s, the first German Lutheran settlers began to migrate into Lavaca County. Some of the families that settled there were: Schott, Fernau, Miller, Strunk, Obelgonner, Fuchs, Laas, Bock, Dryer, and Weller. They settled in a community called Honey Creek—and later called Strunkville since D. Strunk had established a cotton gin and grocery store nearby.

In 1866, Reverend Christopher Gieger, then pastor of Salem

Zion Lutheran Church.

152

Lutheran Church near Brenham, was sent to the Lavaca/ Fayette/Colorado County area as a "traveling missionary." He traveled throughout these counties—and further—conducting worship services whenever and wherever he could, often in homes, schools and sometimes in church buildings of other denominations.

On April 12, 1868, Reverend Gieger organized a congregation at Strunkville. In 1869, he confirmed a class of nineteen adults there. The first church building was dedicated in February, 1870. In May of 1887, it was replaced by a larger building and dedicated as the Zion Evangelical Lutheran Church.

On July 25, 1901, Reverend Gieger died after 34 years of faithful service to the congregation.

In 1887, the SA & AP Railroad was completed from Houston to San Antonio, and a new community, called Sublime, sprang up by the railroad, a few miles south of Strunkville. Gradually, the business—and the population—began to relocate in Sublime. In 1905, the members of Zion Lutheran decided to move their church to Sublime. They dismantled the church, numbering each board, and re-assembled it in Sublime.

In 1928, the congregation voted to have all services—except on the second Sunday of the month—in English.

The Zion Lutheran Church of Sublime continues to function today, in the same building there in the Sublime community, under the leadership of the present pastor, Reverend Herb C. Beyer, Jr. It has never been a large congregation—usually numbering somewhere between forty and seventy members—but it has never faltered in its devotion to duty.

It remains a strong and viable church.

Brewington Baptist Church

HOUSTON COUNTY

"With that bell and those three crosses, it looks impressive."

It is not known, for sure, when the Brewington Baptist Church was established, but deed records show that on March 12, 1909, W. F. Murchison, for the sum of $20, sold 4½ acres to "Green Burnett, Thomas Curvey, Alex Cook, Bill Harris and John Davis, pastor and deacons of the Brewington Baptist Church." It is believed the church had already been in existence for some time—but at different locations.

According to information originally furnished by Mrs. Willie Hayes Roach (and given to Mrs. Ella Curvey Green) the first location of the Brewington Church was on Percilla Road—and that

Brewington Baptist Church.

154

building burned. The second location was about ¼ mile behind the present church and the third church was also located behind the present church. The present building, located east of Grapeland, on CR 1675, is the fourth building. It is believed the church was named for a Rev. Brewer.

According to the information compiled by Mrs. Roach and Mrs. Green, early pastors were Rev. Jim Brown, Rev. Helem, Rev. Hunter, Rev. Issac Waters, Rev. Webb, Rev. Hudson, Rev. Sheilds, Rev. J. W. Walters, Rev. Alexander. Rev. S. A. Keel, Rev. E. L. Little John, Rev. King Mitchell, Rev. Bud Chandler, Rev. Pappy Reese, Rev. Simpson, Rev. E. A. Blackshire, Rev. I. S. Groves, and Rev. Webb Wilson.

Three different nearby creeks—San Pedro Creek, Murchison Creek, and Coppers Branch—are believed to have been used for baptisms at different times.

The present building is an impressive looking one—with the three crosses and the bell in front. Rev. Joe Ard has pastored the church since 1974. The membership has been declining in recent years—as the population in the area has declined. But, as Rev. Ards says, "We've still got some good, faithful members . . . and their church is very important to them—just as it has always been."

Center Hill Methodist Church

HOUSTON COUNTY

"It used to be Corinth."

The Center Hill Methodist Church, located northwest of Kennard, on FM 1733, has a long—and somewhat unusual—history. In 1858, an unordained preacher named Edmund Mason established a church, a cemetery and a school (the school and the church were in the same building) on his land. The church was called the Corinth Methodist Church. Some of the original families were Morgan, Armstrong, Warner and Harrison.

Center Hill Methodist Church.

156

When the War Between the States broke out, Rev. Mason (along with his son) went off to war. When the war ended, and they returned home, there were delinquent taxes on the land . . . the taxes had not been paid while they were away at war. With no cash money available to pay the taxes, Rev. Mason eventually lost the land (and with it, the church) to taxes.

A few years later, the Corinth Church burned. Shortly thereafter, in 1878, the residents of the Corinth, Zion, and Randolph communities combined to form a new church . . . not far away from the old Corinth Church. They called it the Center Hill Methodist Church.

According to research done by Ms. Eliza Bishop, some of the early preachers at the Center Hill Church were W. F. Julian, Robert F. Hodges, E. T. Brasher, Rev. Tunnell, Rev. J. C. Huddleston, and Rev. Charles Lamb. Until sometime in the 1930s, a school was also operated at the site, along with the church.

In 1957, the present church building was constructed, using lumber from the previous building. It is believed this is the fourth building to serve the church.

Gerald Morgan grew up in the Center Hill community, moved away and then returned. "Our membership is pretty small now" says Mr. Morgan. "We're down to about sixteen members . . . but we still have services every Sunday. Our pastor is Rev. Doug Howell—he also pastors the Lovelady church. The Center Hill Church has a rich history . . . and we hope we can keep it going for a long time yet to come."

Vsetin Czech-Moravian Brethren Church

LAVACA COUNTY

"Only six pastors."

Around 1865, Czech people began migrating into Lavaca County (primarily into the eastern portion of the county) and they soon established two communities—Vsetin and Bila Hora. Some of these early families were: Stasny, Holubec, Trlica, Sralla, Dusek, Fojt, Balusek, Melnar, Roznojak, Mikeska, Valchar, and Woytek. Descendants of these families still live in the area.

These settlers soon established schools in both communities. In

1884, a Brethren Moravian preacher by the name of Reverend Henry Jurena preached the first sermon, in the schoolhouse at Bila Hora. Shortly thereafter, Reverend Jurena began preaching regularly at both schools and established congregations in both communities

In 1894, the two groups decided to combine into one and to erect a church building. John Trlica donated two acres of land at Vsetin and thus was born the Vsetin Czech-Moravian Brethren Church. The building was dedicated on April 28, 1895, and it served for the next fifty-nine years.

Vsetin Czech-Moravian Brethren Church, old
—Courtesy of Church

In 1951, the members voted to erect a new building. It was completed in December 1954, utilizing 12,000

Vsetin Czech-Moravian Brethren Church, new
—Courtesy of Church

board feet of lumber salvaged from the old building. That building
still serves today.

In the early 1930s, a Sunday School was formed. Until 1954, all
Sunday School services were conducted in the Czech language.

In its entire history, the church has only had six elected pastors.
Reverend Henry Jurena was the first, followed by Reverend Adolph
Chlumsky, Reverend B. O. Kubricht, Reverend Anton Motycka,
Reverend F. J. Kostohryz, and Reverend Henry Beseda, Jr., who be-
came the full time pastor in 1971 and continues to serve in that ca-
pacity today.

The Vsetin Czech-Moravian Brethren Church continues to
function, sitting there on the side of a hill in the Vsetin
Community, on FMR 2314, northeast of Hallettsville, where it has
been since 1895.

Old Moulton Baptist Church

LAVACA COUNTY

"The town moved . . . but the church stayed."

Located west of Moulton, on FMR 1680, the Old Moulton Baptist Church has a long history. In 1873, there was a split in the membership of the nearby Live Oak Baptist Church and about twenty-five of those members left the Live Oak church and formed a new church—the Old Moulton Baptist Church. "Old Moulton" refers to the original Moulton community. After the railroad later came in, a few miles to the east, most of the community gradually relocated there. The church stayed.

Old Moulton Baptist Church

The building, originally a two story structure, was built in 1873 or 1874. The upper story was used by the Masonic Lodge until about 1894. For many years, the building was also used as a school house. Somewhere around the turn of the century, the upper story was removed. The lower story has been used continuously since 1874. The church is about the only remaining reminder of the Old Moulton Community.

With the relocation of the Moulton community, the population of the Old Moulton area gradually declined . . . and, with it, the membership of the Old Moulton church. Finally, the church closed. There are no longer any regular services held here.

Because of its history—and rich heritage—the church is a popular choice for special occasions—weddings, funerals, etc.

Rocky Mountain Baptist Church

HOUSTON COUNTY

"I'm a third generation member."

Normally, one would not expect to see the name "Rocky Mountain" show up anywhere in East Texas . . . but there it is . . . the Rocky Mountain Baptist Church, located on FM 229, northwest of Crockett. It is believed the name comes from a high hill—or bluff—directly across the road from the church. And, yes, it is indeed somewhat rocky.

Written history of the church is somewhat scarce, but we know the land on which the church sits was given to the church in 1900,

Rocky Mountain Baptist Church

by Pete Nelson. It is believed that Rev. Wallace Porter was the first pastor, and Rev. Martin Reece was the second. Early families included Porter, Newman, Elam, Johnson, Kizzie, and McCullough.

"I grew up in the church" says Mrs. Jo Etta (McCullough) Owens. "I'm a third generation member. My parents—Bill and Katherine McCullough—and my grandmother, Lillie Elam, before me, were active in the church. The church has always been a very important part of my life . . . it always will be."

"Our membership is small now—we don't have many young folks any more—but we're still active. We have services twice a month. Rev. Harold Franklin is our pastor. To those of us that are left, the church is still very, very important to us. It will always be that way."

Ivie Missionary Baptist Church

HOUSTON COUNTY

"They're faithful members—along with two Methodists."

Located south of Kennard, on CR 4645, Ivie Missionary Baptist Church is nestled in a grove of trees. It is not known, for sure, when the church was founded. In 1995, at the age of seventy-two, R. L. Ivie (now deceased) wrote that he had attended church there all his life, as did his father, Leon Ivie (born in 1896). His grandfather, Elisha Ivie, born in 1853, attended church there, but it is not known how far back. Mr. Ivie stated that his great-grandfather, Henry Ivie, was buried there in the cemetery in 1861, but it was not known if the church existed at that time.

There was a spring located behind the church that served as a

Ivie Baptist Church

source of water for many families in the area. It is believed that there was also a school located here at one time.

Mr. Ivie recalled attending outdoor revival meetings, in the 1930s, that sometimes lasted two or three weeks, often conducted by a Rev. Higgenbotham, from Lufkin.

At some point—the date is unknown—there was a division in the church and some of the members left and formed a new church a few miles away, called Old Ivie, and later called Stubblefield.

Somewhere around 1944 or 1945, the old building was torn down and the present one was constructed.

Mrs. Mertis (Gates) Goodson recalls attending the Ivie church as a child. "I grew up there (my paternal grandmother was Mary Ivie). Then we moved away. We moved back in 1991 and my husband and I joined the church in 1994. We're down now to twelve members, but they're all faithful members—and we have two Methodists that worship with us. We still have services every Sunday morning, Sunday night and Wednesday night. Rev. Marshall Jackson comes here every week to conduct our services. The church is still a big part of our lives."

Second Corinth Missionary Baptist Church

WALLER COUNTY

"Still in the original building."

By deed dated February 23, 1884, the Giddings/Stone Plantation owners conveyed one acre of land to James Hill, George Cain, James Thompson and Peter Henderson, Trustees for the Walnut Bayou Missionary Baptist Church. It is believed that the church already existed at that time, and probably had been meeting under a brush arbor and/or in whatever temporary buildings they were able to use. The name came from the Walnut Bayou Creek that ran nearby.

Mrs. Bernice Fuller
—Courtesy of Mrs. Fuller

Located just off FM 1736, northwest of Hempstead on Qualls Road, it is believed this is the original structure still standing on that one acre tract. Sometime between 1909 and 1913, the name of the church was changed to the Second Corinth Missionary Baptist Church. Records indicate that in those early years, the church had a membership of up to thirty-five members. In 1910, the pastor was Rev. E. L. Lock. There is no record of who may have served as pastor before that date.

As was common with many community churches in those days,

Second Corinth Baptist Church

the Walnut Bayou Church built and operated a school, adjacent to the church and taught classes in that school for many years.

"I'm eighty-five, and I've been a member of the Second Corinth Church all my life" says Mrs. Bernice Fuller. "The church was always the center of our community. This has always been my church ... and it still is."

The Second Corinth Church still functions today, under the leadership of Rev. Cube Charleston, in that original building. The church is still a focal point of the community ... just as it has been since 1884.

Mt. Olive Missionary Baptist Church

HOUSTON COUNTY

"My Mama was a member for ninety-three years."

We've both been members of the Mt. Olive Church all our lives," says Mrs. Mattie B. (Williams) Bailey." "I'm seventy-seven and Booker is eighty-four . . . we've both been members for as long as we can remember. Our parents before us were members."

"My Mama was a member for ninety-three years . . . she was 105 when she died, in 1998," adds Mr. Booker T. Bailey. "Our grandparents—both of us—were members too, but we don't know for how long. I grew up there, close to the church. I was away during World

Mr. and Mrs. Booker Bailey

168

Mrs. Lillie Bailey on her one-hundredth birthday
—Courtesy of Mr. Bailey

War II, while I was in the Army, but, other than that, I've been here all my life."

"I grew up here in town (Lovelady)," says Mrs. Bailey, "but I've always belonged to the Mt. Olive Church. This area—and this church—has always been home to us."

Of the three Mt. Olive Baptist churches in Houston County, this one, located on CR 3545, southwest of Lovelady, is known as the "Lower Mt. Olive Church." The church's early history is very sketchy. It is believed that at some point, many years ago, the church records were lost in a fire. It is known that there was originally a church "out on 230" many, many years ago, and at some point, there was a split in that church. No one remembers the reasons for the split. The Mt. Olive Church was formed as a result of that split, but no one knows when that happened. The present building is about fifty years old, but it is not the original building.

Some of the early families were Burnett, Bailey, Darden, Jones,

Mt. Olive Baptist Church

Jackson, Armstead, Hutchins, Stubblefield, Williams, Griffin, McKnight, York, Wiley, Phillips, Strange, Minor, Wingwood, Horace, and Kings.

Although the list is probably incomplete, some of the early pastors were Rev. Wm. D. Hemphill, Rev. Stephens, Rev. Perry, Rev. Bradford, Rev. W. E. Jones, Rev. J. H. Hill, Rev. E. G. Byrd, Rev. Jesse Jones, Rev. Bates, and Rev. Frank Wagner.

Mr. Bailey, presently a deacon in the church, points to the list of deacons, "My grandfather, Alfred Bailey, was a deacon." Other deacons on the list are: Julius Bailey, Jorden Bailey, Robert Bailey, Pullian Bailey, Davis Howard, Earl Howard, John Street, Jack Darden, Boyd McKnight, and L. H. Griffin.

"Our membership is small now" says Mr. Bailey. "We don't have many young folks anymore . . . but we still have church every Sunday . . . and we have a big Homecoming program on the 4th Sunday of every August. Our pastor now is Rev. Laurence Sowell.

"Both of us still attend church on a regular basis. We've been doing that, every Sunday, all our lives . . . and as long we're able, we're going to keep doing it . . . that's our church!!!"

Siloam Baptist Church

LEON COUNTY

"The old church book burned."

The early history of the Siloam Baptist Church, located between Centerville and Buffalo, is somewhat vague, because, as
stated in an old Trinity River Baptist Association book, "The old
church book was burned." It is believed the church was organized
by M. M. Haggard and Johnnie Brown. Although we don't know
for sure, it is believed the year was 1876. Those same Trinity River
Association records show the following: "In 1885, S. P. Cummings
was called as pastor and J. C. Talden, church clerk . . . The third
Sunday in 1885, Rev. Smiley Neyland preached. D. C. Dove, Jr. was
clerk . . . In 1886, D. M. McKay was pastor . . . G. G. Dove joined
the church in 1876 and D. C. Dove, Jr. joined in July, 1884."

According to Mrs. Cheryl (Swarthout) Burks, who—along
with her mother, Mrs. Joyce Swarthout—has done extensive research on the history of the Siloam Church, "My great-grandparents, Oscar Beggs, Sr. and Alice Alexander McNellege, were
married in the Siloam Church August 1, 1894. My grandparents,
Leonard T. Ridenour and Victoria Beggs, were also married here
October 8, 1924. On February 13, 1993, I was married to Kerry
Burks, in the Siloam Church."

In a deed dated in 1905, Mrs. Arcanum Summrall, widow of
Jesse Sumrall, donated the land on which the church is located.
However, the wording of the deed indicates that the church was already in existence at that time, at that same location, as was the
cemetery and a school. It is known that Mrs. Sumrall had taught
school at the Siloam school in 1870 and 1871. According to an obit-
uary written in 1919, by S. A. Castles, Mrs. Sumrall, born in

171

Mississippi, in 1841 (her maiden name was Gustine) married Jesse Sumrall in 1857. He served in the Confederate Army and was wounded—and captured—in 1863. He was sent to a northern hospital as a prisoner of war. Upon learning of her husband's fate, Mrs. Summrall, alone, crossed enemy lines and made her way to that hospital, and nursed and cared for her husband until he was later paroled and exchanged. They moved to Texas in 1865, and settled where the Siloam Church now stands. Mrs. Sumrall joined the Siloam Church in 1876—it appears likely that she was a charter member. She is buried in the Siloam Cemetery, beside her husband.

According to those same Trinity River Association book, early pastors at Sioam included J. L. Blackwell, J. M. Peters, W J. Kenedy, E. A. Puthuff, J. T. Marsh, Rev. Harris, W. T. Chase, C. J. Stevens, E. N. Parrish, Rev. Shaw, E. R. Bilderback, John Lutwyler, and T. F. Suttle. The present church building is the original structure . . . built in 1876, or shortly thereafter.

In 1905, there was a split—or division—within the Siloam Church, and some of the members left and formed the nearby Social Grove Baptist Church. Any study of the history of old Baptist churches indicates that such splits were not particularly uncommon in those early days.

Siloam Baptist Church

Although the Siloam Church was a vital part of the community, it has functioned sporadically in recent years. In the late 1940s, due to a declining rural population, the church closed. It was resurrected and re-opened sometime in the mid-1950s. It continued to function until 1960 . . . we think (the last entry in the minute book is dated October, 1960) . . . when it closed again. In 1984, the Siloam Church was resurrected . . . again. It functioned until 1999, when it closed again.

The Siloam Church is used today only for special occasions . . . in 2000, Michael Wayne Swarthout and Lasonna Lucille (Lawson) Drummond were married in the church. At the present time, the building is being used, on a temporary basis, by another congregation.

The old Siloam Baptist Church building still sits there, where it has been for over 126 years. As Mrs. Swarthout and Mrs. Burks put it, "There are so many, many memories there. The church was so important to this community for so many, many years. This church was founded on love for God and fellow man and you can still feel that love today whether the building is being used or not."

Who knows? . . . perhaps it will be resurrected again, one of these days.

Mt. Olive Missionary Baptist Church (Middle)

HOUSTON COUNTY

"Yes, this is the middle one."

There are three Mt. Olive Baptist churches in Houston County. This particular one, located south of Crockett, on CR 4020, is known as the "Middle Mt. Olive Church."

The church burned in 1946, destroying all the church records, so the early history of the church is somewhat lacking. In 1979, one of the older members, Mrs. Millie Ann Williams (now deceased) wrote down all she could remember of the church history. According to her, the church had its beginning about 1883, in the

Mt. Olive Baptist Church (old)

—Courtesy of Church

174

Mt. Olive Baptist Church, new

home of Jim Crowder—a one room log building with a dirt floor. It was later moved to the home of Jiel Huntley. At this time, the church was known as the Macedonia Missionary Baptist Church.

According to Mrs. Williams, in 1898, Alex Davis and his wife, Rosa Cook Davis donated one acre of land at a location closer to the center of the community—and on a better road—and the church was relocated there (this is the present site). At the same time, the name was changed to the Mt. Olive Missionary Baptist Church. For many years, a school was operated at this same site.

It is believed the first pastor (and founder) was Rev. Raefield Cotton. The church has had several pastors who have served well through the years, including one—Rev. A. C. Harris—who served for forty years.

Another whose name shows up repeatedly through the years was Rev. Cojo Harris. He served, at various times as community minister, Sunday school superintendent, church secretary and teacher at the school.

In 1993, the outside of the church was bricked up, preserving the original structure. The church today, has a fairly stable membership and under the leadership of the present pastor, Rev. Laverne Gambrell, has services every Sunday.

Salem Baptist Church

LAVACA COUNTY

"It had six members."

There is some uncertainty as to the date of the birth of the Salem Baptist Church. The earliest record in the minutes of the church indicates August 6, 1859. However, the minutes of the Guadalupe Association indicate Salem was organized in 1857. Either way, Salem is a very, very old church. At its organization, it had only six members. Its first pastor is believed to have been Reverend W. H. Holland.

The original building burned about 1874. It was replaced immediately. In 1902, the present structure was built and continues to serve.

Records indicate that Sunday School was begun in 1902. Over the years, the church has sent six of its members into the ministry:

Salem Baptist Church

H. C. Crocker, Thomas Reagan, James Swenburg, George Kimball, Donald Cook, and Kenneth Hodges.

Some years ago, Salem Baptist started a tri-yearly gospel music event. Held on the second Sunday of February, June and October, it has proven to be a very popular event, attracting visitors from all over.

Located on FMR 531, in the Ezzell community, about thirteen miles south of Hallettsville, the Salem church has served the community for over 140 years now. Although small in numbers, under the leadership of Reverend Leon Smothers, it continues to function as a vibrant, full-time church.

/ŀt. Pleasant Baptist Church

FORT BEND COUNTY

"Reverend Randle . . . he died on the job."

Sometime in 1878, the Reverend London Branch, pastor of the Mt. Carmel Baptist Church, in Richmond (Fort Bend County), along with a few of his members, traveled to the nearby Booth community to help organize a new church there. They decided to call it the Mt. Pleasant Baptist Church. Reverend G. W. Smith, a member of the Mt. Carmel Church, became the first pastor of the new church. Reverend Smith would go on to pastor the church for 54 years.

Services were apparently held wherever they could find an avail-

Mt. Pleasant Baptist Church

178

Rev. Smith and Rev. Lampley

able place for several years. Finally, in 1894, they built a church. In 1900, a terrible, terrible storm moved through Fort Bend County, destroying many buildings. The Mt. Pleasant Church was one of the casualties of the storm, being completely destroyed. Finally, in 1903, a replacement building was finished. It's still there, in the same location, on Jones River Road, a short distance south of Booth.

Rev. Randle and Rev. Jones

The Mt. Pleasant Church has had several notable pastors over the years—among them Rev. Smith, Rev. J. L. Lampley, Rev. W. S. Autrey, Rev. A. W. Johnson, Rev. W. R. Jones, Rev. R. M. Randle and Rev. Ned Walker.

Reverend Randle, who had pastored the church for over fourteen years, died "on the job," so to speak, in 1969. While preaching at the nearby Mt. Zion Baptist Church, he died in the pulpit, from an apparent heart attack.

The Mt. Pleasant Baptist Church, under the leadership of its current pastor, Reverend Leroy Houston, recently celebrated its 150th anniversary. It is in an area of drastic growth. New subdivisions are springing up all around it. Directly across the road is a new golf course. No one knows what the future holds as the area continues to grow. For the time being, however, the Mt. Pleasant Baptist Church continues to function as one of the stronger and more stable of the old country churches—much as it has for more than 150 years.

Harmony Baptist Church

GRIMES COUNTY

"They built it on Harmony Hill."

Sometime in the mid-1850s, John Moore McGinty and his wife, Mary Loretta (Brown) McGinty organized a Baptist church in the Grimes Prairie area, north of Stoneham. They called it the Grimes Prairie Baptist Church. Records show the church existed at least as early as 1857. In that year, the membership was twenty-seven, and the pastor was Rev. J. F. Hillyear.

By 1859, there had been some changes in population patterns and the church was moved to its present location, about six miles northeast of Navasota, north of Hwy 105, on what was then called Harmony Lane. With the move, it was renamed "Harmony Baptist

Harmony Baptist Church

Church." It is believed that Rev. John Moore was the first pastor in the new location.

Other early pastors included Rev. J. M. Perry, Rev. F. M. Law, Rev. J. H Stribbling, Rev. J. T. Zealy, Rev. W. H. Dodson, Rev. C Felder, Rev. G. M. Daniel, Rev. Rugus Figh, Rev. B. B. Williams, Rev. J. M. Dodson, Rev. J. F. Dobbs, Rev. R. J. McGinty, Rev. E. B. Hearn, Rev. B. Broome, Rev. W. H. Jones, Rev. J. L. Fuqua, and Rev. J. N. Clayton.

For awhile, they held services in a school house (not an uncommon situation). In 1870, they erected a church building. It served until around 1924, when the present building was erected, built partially of wood from the old building.

Due to a declining population in the area, regular services were discontinued some years ago, but the building is still used occasionally for special events, including an annual homecoming. It serves as a reminder of "days gone by," when life was good on Harmony Lane there by Harmony Hill.

Lynn Grove Methodist Church

GRIMES COUNTY

"The church was the center of our community life."

In 1888, a group of settlers, south of Navasota, in the Lynn Grove Community, decided they needed a church—so they formed one—and they called it the Lynn Grove Methodist Church.

Some of the early families were Weaver, Shine, Lewis, Hammons, and Mitchell. According to Benford Weaver, a life-long member of the church, "My family has always been involved in this church. My grandfather, Z. S. Weaver, was one of the original trustees."

Located at 16402 CR 310, south of Navasota, the church has

Lynn Grove Methodist Church

183

functioned continuously ever since, even though there was a period during the 1930s when they didn't have a preacher for awhile. The present building was built in 1947.

As Mr. Weaver puts it, "The church was the center of our community life for so many, many years. Everything revolved around the church. The church was the center of our social life, as well as of our religious life. The church was the most important factor in our lives."

Like so many small country churches, Lynn Grove dwindled in numbers during the post WW II era, but revived somewhat in later years.

Now, once again, the numbers are small—but the church still functions regularly, holding services every Sunday. "There are so many, many memories here" says Mr. Weaver. "The church has been so very, very important to us for so many years—particularly for us older folks. The church is still very dear to us. I think it always will be."

Ratcliff Baptist Church

HOUSTON COUNTY

"I've been a member for about eighty years."

"I joined the Ratcliff Baptist Church when I was in my early teens . . . and I'm ninety-four now . . . so I've probably been a member for about eighty years." Mrs. May Killion was recounting her relationship with the Ratcliff Baptist Church.

"I was always told the church was organized in about 1904 and that Henry Rudd and Dr. Ben Barclay helped organize it" she said. It is believed the first building was built in 1912 by the Four C Mill, which was at that time one of the largest sawmills west of the Mississippi River. It is believed the building was moved once

Ratcliff Baptist Church

185

(around 1920) to the Ratcliff area and later, after damage from a windstorm, was moved to its present location, on Hwy 7, near FM 227. It appears the church originally functioned as a union church (not uncommon in those early days) serving several denominations, but eventually evolved into solely a Baptist church. It is not known when the present building was built.

"We don't have as many members as we used to" says Mrs. Killion, but we still have two services every Sunday and prayer meeting every Wednesday night. The church has always been a very, very important part of our lives. It has always been important to me. I've been blessed with good health . . . and I've only missed two Sundays since 1974."

Under the leadership of the present pastor, Rev. Kenneth Wooley, the Ratcliff Baptist Church continues to serve the needs of the community—and of its members. As Mrs. Killion puts it, "The church has always been there when we needed it. I hope it'll be there for a long time still to come."

Midway Missionary Baptist Church

GRIMES COUNTY

"It burned on a Sat. night . . . and they had church the next morning."

According to the best information available, in 1883, V. C. Nowlin donated a parcel of land, for church purposes, to Deacons Prince Birdwell, Nora Lewis, Jack Gooden, Henry Haynes, Sam Davis, Peter Moore and Henry Dickey. The following year, 1884, the Midway Missionary Baptist Church was organized. The first pastor was Rev. Henry Williams and the deacons were Nora Lewis and Prince Birdwell.

Another early pastor was Rev. Cornelius Harris.

According to long time member, Booker Parkhill, Sr., eighty-five, "I've been a member of the Midway Church since 1942 . . . I'm

Booker Parkhill

a deacon now. It's my understanding the church burned in 1916, on a Saturday night. They held services the next morning in the schoolhouse nearby. The church was rebuilt a short distance from the original one.

"The church has always been an important part of our community life . . . it has always been there when we needed it. It helped teach our young folks right and wrong and how to behave.

"The building we've got now is the third building. We don't have many folks anymore—only about

187

Midway Baptist Church.

twelve or thirteen members—but we still have services once a month—on the third Sunday. The church is still real important to us old-timers."

Located at the dead-end of a private lane just off FM 2620, northeast of Shiro, the old Midway Missionary Baptist Church is still there, serving as a reminder of days gone by.

Mt. Zion Missionary Baptist Church

GRIMES COUNTY

"We've been here for 131 years . . . we'll be here a while longer."

In August 1871, a small group of folks in the Courtney Community, south of Navasota, decided they needed a church. Under the leadership of Rev. Prince Keil, they decided to do something about it—they organized a church. Others involved in that early effort were Anthony Thornton, R. M. Thomas, N. B. Sparks, J. A. West, Frank Hendricks, O. Boone, and Harry Ross.

In March 1872, they moved into their new building—small though it was—located on south side of what is now FM 2. This building served until 1947 when, needing a larger facility, under the leadership of Rev. Robert Cunningham, they bought an old home

Mt. Zion Missionary Baptist Church

and renovated and remodeled it to serve as a sanctuary. That building is still in use today, on the north side of FM 2.

Like so many country churches, the Mt. Zion Church has had
to contend, in recent years, with a declining population in the area.
"Our congregation is small" says Mrs. Debra Steptoe, "but we've
got some good, solid folks, and the church is still important to all
of us. It's an important part of our lives—just like it has been for
more than 130 years."

Under the leadership of the current pastor, Rev. Bennie Steptoe,
the Mt. Zion Church still functions, on a regular basis—and expects
to continue to do so for some time yet.

Pilgrim Point Missionary Baptist Church

GRIMES COUNTY

"It has served five generations of my family."

Like many of the old, small country churches, the Pilgrim Point Missionary Baptist Church began functioning before it had a building of its own. It was organized in 1915 and began holding services in a small one room school house named Post Oak Spring School. According to the present church secretary, Mrs. Yvonne (Manning) Toston, some of the original charter members were Amos Dunn, Mittie Manning, Charlie Reese and Carrie Lofton.

The first pastor, on an interim basis, was Rev. P. H. Johnson. The first permanent pastor was Rev. Lawson Allen.

Mrs. Earnestine Manning and great-grandchildren.
—Courtesy of Mrs. Toston

At one time, services were held in the Home Benefit Society Building. Finally, in 1940, the church bought one acre of land, and erected their first building, located on CR 446, east of Navasota. That structure still stands—and still serves—today.

The Manning family has been one of the foundation families throughout the life of the church. According to Mrs. Toston, "My grandmother, Mittie Manning, was one of the original charter members; my parents, Norwood and Earnestine Manning, were members virtually all their lives; and I've been a member since 1947. My eleven brothers and sisters were all members, my children were members, and my grandson, T. J., is a member. My brother, Rickey Manning, is the present pastor. My mother, Ernestine Manning, is the oldest member (she's eighty-eight)."

Mrs. Yvonne Toston and grandchildren
—Courtesy of Mrs. Toston

Under the leadership of Rev. Manning, the Pilgrim Point Church still functions as a small, but active church, serving the needs of its people—and of the community. As Mrs. Toston puts it, "This church been a huge part of our lives for five generations. We hope it remains this way for a long, long time to come."

Pilgrim Point Baptist Church.

More Churches

Parker Chapel AME Church, Austin County

Sweet Cornersville Baptist Church, Ft. Bend County

Anderson Chapel Methodist Church, Houston County

Harper Methodist Church, Waller County

Shady Grove Baptist Church

HOUSTON COUNTY

"Collection taken for Orphan's Home . . . $16.10 was collected."

Very little information could be found pertaining to the early history of the Shady Grove Baptist Church. Located southeast of Crockett, on Hwy 287, the church is believed to have been organized around 1876, but very little is known about those early years.

Minutes covering a period of years, beginning in 1908, were found, and given to Mrs. Delmer Woolley. These minutes give us some insight into what took place in the church during a period of about twenty-five years. Mrs. Woolley has provided these excerpts from those minutes.

"Oct. 10, 1908: Business meeting. After devotional, Bro. John

Shady Grove Baptist Church.

195

B. Satterwhite, E C. Satterwhite, and A.B. Hallmark were elected as messengers to the association."

"June, 1908: Bro. Carter was requested to preach at night on 'The Church.'"

"Bro. C. B. Hallmark and W. H. Satterwhite was ordained as deacons on May 8, 1909."

"Aug. 7, 1909, W. H. Satterwhite was licensed to preach the gospel . . . Met to begin a protracted meeting which lasted nine days. On the tenth day 10 were baptized and five joined by statement."

"Collection for Buckner Orphan's Home was taken on Oct. 18, 1910. $16.10 was collected."

"Minutes of Aug. 24, 1929 stated that it had been years since the church had a held a business meeting. A revised church roll showed 42 resident members."

"Sept. 1, 1935: Claude Woolley, Allen Woolley, Dewy Smith, and Earl Satterwhite was ordained as deacons. Doyle McCelvey was ordained to preach the gospel."

Mrs. Woolley notes "Allen Woolley was my father-in-law. I wish we had more information on the history of the church—but that's all we have been able to find."

The Shady Grove Baptist Church—located in that same shady grove—continues to function, under the leadership of the present pastor, Rev. Paul Carlin.

Pleasant Grove Baptist Church

GRIMES COUNTY

"It molded my value system and my moral standards."

The early history of the Pleasant Grove Baptist Church is somewhat sketchy, but it is believed the church was first organized around 1875, when one of the original members, Mose Lawrence, donated land for church purposes. For several years, the church was referred to as the Mose Lawrence Church—and later the name was changed to its present name—the Pleasant Grove Baptist Church.

The first pastor was a Rev. Rinehart. It is believed that in the early years, they worshipped under a brush arbor for an undeter-

Pleasant Grove Baptist Church

197

mined period before they finally had a building. Rev. Willie Hall was the second pastor of the church. In those early years, the church was located in a community called Black Jack. Other pastors were Rev. B. J. Collins, Rev. W. M. Griffin, Rev. L. T. Ward, Rev. W. A. Johnson, Rev. J. P. Davis, Rev. L. E. Turner, Rev. W. P. Powell, and Rev. C. L. Corner.

The first deacons of the church were George Henry, Jack Debose, Billy Bell, Lynch Ward, and Mose Lawrence. The present deacons are Louis Taylor, Robert Taylor, Asian Ford, Jackson Glover and Lee Andrew Mason.

In 1935, the church moved to its present location, a few miles northeast of Navasota, on CR 446.

"I grew up in this church" says Mrs. Jackie Glover, Ass't Sec. of the church. "I joined the church when I was about five or six years old and I was a member till I turned eighteen and moved away . . . I was away for twenty-one years until I moved back in 1998. This church played a big part in influencing the development of my belief system and in shaping and molding my value system and my moral standards."

Like most country churches, the Pleasant Grove Church has been through its ups and downs over the years, but in the last 21 years, under the leadership of Rev. James Lee, the church has grown in numbers and has become—again—a strong, stable church.

Mt. Zion Ash Baptist Church

HOUSTON COUNTY

"In 1942, they were paying on it . . . to Smith-Murchison."

There is little written record of the history of the Mt. Zion Ash Baptist Church, located on CR 3230, southeast of Crockett.

Ms. Jessie Murphy, who grew up in the community, and attended church there as a child, has a limited amount of information from an old ledger that belonged to her father, Hal Murphy. He was one of the original deacons—along with Jim Buckner, Grover Warren, and John Pruitt.

According to Ms. Murphy, "We don't know, for sure, when the church was built. We know Mose Sherman gave two acres of land

Mt. Zion Ash Baptist Church.

199

for the church . . . and we think they probably worshipped under a brush arbor for awhile. My father's old ledger shows that, in 1942, they were paying on it. They were making payments to Smith-Murchison Lumber and Hardware. Smith-Murchison apparently supplied the materials for the church, and was carrying a note on it. So, we think the church was probably built around 1940 or 1941.

"I can't find any record of who the first pastor was. One of the early ones was a Rev. Burnett, who came in here from Louisiana and pastored the church for a long time."

Like so many of the country churches, the membership has dropped in recent years—as has the population in the area. But, to those that are left, the church is still very important to them. They still have Sunday School every Sunday, and preaching about once a month.

"Raven Sherman, a great-grandson of Mose Sherman, kind of keeps the place up," says Ms. Murphy, "and he preaches sometimes."

Once a year, in August, the church has an all-day Homecoming event and as Ms Murphy puts it "Everybody comes back home to Mt. Zion Ash Church."

Monaville Baptist Church

WALLER COUNTY

"Lots of changes . . . names and places."

The Monaville Baptist Church, presently located at Schmidt Road and Richard Frey Road, east of Monaville, has been through more than one location—and more than one name—since its beginning.

Organized about 1908, it was originally called the Harris Creek Baptist Church. It was built on the banks of a small creek by the same name. We don't know who the first pastor was, but the first two deacons were Jack Hopkins and Allen Nichols.

According to information furnished by Mrs. Ruth Ellis, the

Monaville Baptist Church

J. R. Richardson, Susan Bagley, Richard Sykula, Jack DeLozier, Curtis Pietrowski, and J. J. Davis

—Courtesy of Mrs. Ruth Ellis

Richard Sykula, Rev. Mike Garrett, J. R. Richardson, and Susan Bagley.

—Courtesy of Mrs. Ruth Ellis

church secretary, the church remained at this location until 1931, when it was moved to a spot on the George Bonner Estate. It functioned there until about 1937 or 1938, when membership had declined so much that the church was closed.

It remained closed until, in 1941, it was reorganized under the leadership of a new pastor, Rev. Blankenship. In 1946, the church purchased land from the Monaville Methodist Church and moved the building to this new location.

In 1953, the church was struck by lightening and burned to the ground. For the next two years, services were held in temporary quarters. In 1955, the property at the old location was traded to Mr. John Schmidt for two acres where the church is now located. A new church was built—now the Monaville Baptist Church—at this location and continues to serve today.

In a very unusual side-note, the Monaville Church now has several members who regularly come to church by horseback—J. R. Richardson, Susan Bagby, Richard Sykula, Jack De Lozier, Curtis Pietrowski, and J. J. Davis. There's no particular reason for this . . . they just like to ride horses. The sight of several horses tied up outside on a Sunday morning brings back lots of memories.

The Monaville Baptist Church appears today to be a fairly strong and stable church. The present pastor is Rev. Mike Garrett . . . he has pastored the church for fourteen years. Hopefully, the Monaville Baptist Church has found its spot . . . and will be here from now on.

St. Matthews Baptist Church

HOUSTON COUNTY

"I wish we knew more about its past."

There is little written information regarding the early history of the St. Matthews Baptist Church, located on Hwy. 7, west of Crockett.

It is believed the church was originally called the Haile Baptist Church. It is not known when the present name was adopted.

According to what little information that could be located, the church was organized in 1895, by Joe Uniouns and Ned Uniouns. Pastors between 1895 and 1976 were listed as Rev. Joe Smith, Rev. Champ Newman, Rev. Edd Steptoe, Rev. Jim Jurdens, Rev. Robb

St. Matthews Baptist Church

Groves, Rev. Martin Reace, Rev. A. R. Reace (son of Martin Reace), Rev. H. Mitchell, Rev. H. L. Lewis, Rev. C. C. Sims, and a Rev. Woodall.

Early deacons listed were Primeas Pokes, Addison Houston, Jurdan Wyann, Mack Vaughn, John Morton, John Menfield, and Matthew McDaniel.

The present building was constructed around 1980. The building it replaced is still there, and now serves as the church cafeteria.

The present pastor, Rev. Elliott Reagans, has served the church for 14 years. "I don't know much about the past history of the church" says Rev. Reagans. "My father-in-law, Elbert Warren, was a deacon here—he died when he was ninety-six—but he never wrote down any of the history of the church. We have services every Sunday. We have a membership of about fifty—and it's pretty stable. We have a good many young folks in the church, but not as many as we would like to have.

"Like all the small country churches, we struggle at times, but we're hanging in there. This church is still very, very important to these folks . . . and we're going to do everything we possibly can to make sure the church continues to meet their needs."

Pleasant Hill Baptist Church

GRIMES COUNTY

"It burned three times."

In February, 1894, a small but devoted group of settlers got together and formed a church, a few miles southeast of Navasota, at the dead-end of what is now CR 340. They named it the Pleasant Hill Baptist Church—probably because it is located on a hill, in what certainly would be considered a pleasant location.

The first pastor was Rev. George West and the first deacons were Alex Nelson, George Pratt, Premise Richardt, and Wade Burrell.

Pleasant Hill Baptist Church

According to Mrs. Emma West, a lifelong member, the church has burned three times. "The first building burned in 1913," says Mrs. West. "It was rebuilt . . . and that building burned—we don't know when. They rebuilt again . . . and that one burned in 1940. They were refilling the kerosene lamps, and a small child ran by and knocked over one of the lamps. The lamp broke, the kerosene spilled out and caught fire . . . and the building burned."

The present building replaced the one that burned in that 1940 fire.

Like so many country churches, the congregation is dwindling . . . and aging. "We're down now to about 12 to 15 faithful members now" says Mrs. West. "But, we're doing everything we can—along with our pastor, Rev. Hubert Williams, to maintain our faith—and our church."

Spring Seat Methodist Church

LEON COUNTY

"Or is it Spring Creek . . . or maybe something else?"

In 1884, a group of former slaves living in the Spring Creek Community, in Leon County, decided they needed a church. Like most similar communities in the South, there had been a great deal of uncertainty and turmoil in the years immediately after Emancipation. It took awhile for the freed slaves to adjust to their new circumstances.

Spring Creek was no exception. But by the early 1880s, things had somewhat stabilized. The folks who were living there were farming and raising their families. They expected to be there for a long, long time. Accordingly, they felt the need for a church in their community.

In May 1884, the church had its beginning. Three brothers, Wesley, James, and Edmund Robinson—along with their brother-in-law, Robert Benson—owned a sizeable tract of land in the community. These four men (we believe they had moved there from Alabama, after Emancipation) gave one acre of land for a church. Thus was born the Spring Seat Methodist Church. These four men composed the first Board of Trustees. We have no record of who may have been the first pastor.

There is a great deal of uncertainty about the origins of the church's name. The community in which it is located is known as the Spring Creek Community (because of the creek, by the same name, that runs through the community). The church cemetery, located a couple of miles away, is known as the Spring Creek Cemetery. Yet the church was named Spring Seat. No one seems to know why. There is some speculation (unconfirmed) that it is somehow related to the strong spring of water located nearby. Perhaps there was a bench or seat that had been placed there. Or perhaps there was an old spring seat from a wagon or buggy that was there in a very visible location. Mrs. Coque Campbell, the current church Treasurer, has done extensive research on the history of the church. Says Mrs. Campbell, "We just don't know where the name came from . . . we'll probably never know."

We have no record of whether they had a permanent building, during those early years. It may be that they worshiped under a brush arbor. At any rate, according to Mrs. Campbell's research, in 1901 they erected a building. The Trustees at that time were Ed Mayes, Robert Benson, Davis Johnson, and Dorsey Johnson. Some of the early pastors were Rev. Mans, Rev. Grisby, Rev. Luster, Rev. Young, Rev. Marshall, Rev. Carter, Rev. Gauge, Rev. Cole, Rev. Machvene, and Rev. Titus. In 1956, the present building was erected—Pete Hayden and Jim Smith were the carpenters. The Trustees at that time were Perry Kelly, Wiley Kelley, Jesse Johnson, M. J. Robinson, Joe Rom Mayes, Leamond Lankford, and McKinley Robinson.

Over the years, the Spring Seat Church has sent six of its sons into the ministry—Fred Mayes, Lusk Johnson, Arnett Lankford, Arthur L. Johnson, Robert Johnson, and T. A. Johnson.

As an interesting side-note, in the vacant field, behind the

Spring Seat Methodist Church.

church (a part of the church property) is the largest colony of Scarlet Penstemon (Penstemon murrayanus) the author has ever seen. While not endangered, this gorgeous wildflower (one of nature's most beautiful and striking in appearance) is not particularly common. In late spring, this field (an acre or more) is covered with these beautiful scarlet flowers, being worked by hundreds of hummingbirds and butterflies. No one ever did anything to cause these flowers to be here . . . they just came in on their own. It is a truly gorgeous sight and has been described as "a tribute to the beauty and majesty of the Lord."

"Oh, come to the church in the Wildwood, to the trees where the wildflowers bloom."

Located on CR 420, southwest of Centerville, the Spring Seat Methodist Church still functions, although their numbers are small. Under the leadership of the present pastor, Rev. Obie Groom, they have preaching services once a month—and they try to have some kind of worship service each Sunday. There's not many folks left (almost every one of those remaining is a descendent of the original Robinson families), but they work hard at keeping the church active. The church is still very, very important to these folks, even if we're not sure where that name came from.

St. Martinsville Missionary Baptist Church

GRIMES COUNTY

"Press forward, in view of the past."

It is believed the St. Martinsville Missionary Baptist Church was first organized in 1876, by Rev. Charlie Warren, with the help of Bob Gibbs, Sam Webb, Andrew Grice, Henry Mitchell and Solomon Gray. Their first building was a crude log structure. It was sometime later that they erected a plain wood frame building and actually named the church. Rev. Warren served as the first pastor.

Located east of Navasota at the intersection of Hwy 105 and FM 362, the church has functioned continuously for 126 years. A number of ministers have led the church during this period, among them: Rev. George West, Rev. Branch, Rev. Willie Hall, Rev. J.

St. Martinsville Baptist Church

211

Tabbs, Rev. Parker, and Rev. R. C. Johnson. In 1931, under the leadership of Rev. P. D. Davis, the building was torn down and rebuilt, with Joe Williams, Sam McGinty, Mark Jones, Solomon Miller—along with their wives—doing most of the work. It was sometime after that when the building was moved to its present location—previously it had been located across the creek.

Rev. Davis, after many years of service, was succeeded by Rev. Westbrook, who served well, until his death some years later. He, in turn, was succeeded by Rev. M. L. Durden. It was under Rev. Durden's leadership, in 1966, that the church was again rebuilt, with Deacon Ruben Warren doing much of the work.

Under the leadership of Rev. Raymond Lenton, pastor since 1994, the St. Martinsville Church has grown and added new members in recent years. The church holds services every Sunday. With their current deacons—Phillip "Pop" Arrington, Lucius McDonald, Lea T. Williams, William Arrington, Gerald Peavy, L. C. Cration, and Lawrence Newsome—the church continues to "Press forward, in view of the past."

More Churches

Greater Wade's Chapel Baptist Church, Waller County

New Zion Baptist Church, Leon County

Little Zion Jerusalem Baptist Church, Wharton County

Allen Chapel AME Church, Houston County

St. Paul Baptist Church

GRIMES COUNTY

"We've got a strong Sunday School . . . with about thirty children."

The St. Paul Baptist Church, located on CR 415, east of Navasota, was formed in 1885. Among the early families were Johnson, Louder, Perry, Warren, Tillis, Seymore, Young and Mitchell. The first pastor is believed to have been Rev. Charlie Warren.

According to Mrs. Georgia Loudd, a lifelong member of the church, the original location was about three miles out of Navasota, at an old campground. It later was moved about two miles farther east . . . and in 1947, was moved to its present location.

Apparently, the church has functioned continuously, although

St. Paul Baptist Church

like so many others, it has struggled at times. Under the current leadership of Rev. Jimmy Lawrence, the church is holding its own—and then some.

As Mrs. Loudd puts it, "The St. Paul Church has always been a very, very important part of our lives—the center of our community. We don't have as many folks as we used to, but we're doing okay. We're unusual in that we have a very strong Sunday School . . . we have about thirty children in our church. We have about sixty members altogether. We hope to remain a strong, strong church for a long, long time."

Anderson Baptist Church

GRIMES COUNTY

"It used to be out in the country."

One could argue that the Anderson Baptist Church is not a country church—it's located in the town of Anderson—and that would probably be a legitimate argument. But . . . it used to be out in the country. Back when Rev. Morrell organized it, back in 1844, it was way out in the country.

Rev. Z. N. Morrell was a traveling (by horseback) Baptist preacher/missionary/circuit rider active throughout a wide area of Texas, in the 1840s (when Texas was still a republic). In his book

Anderson Baptist Church

Flowers and Fruits in the Wilderness, Rev. Morrell discusses the formation of the Anderson Church. "During the year 1844," recounts Rev. Morrell, "We kept up a regular appointment at a little school house, with a dirt floor, four miles north of the present locality of Anderson, Grimes County, in the neighborhood of A. G. Perry. Here we gathered together a few Baptists, who petitioned for an

217

organization, and on the 11th day of November 1844, the present church at Anderson was organized . . . with seven members. While the members lived near the school house, we foresaw that in consequence of the rich lands south, the centre of populance would be at "Fanthrop's—now Anderson—and the church was constituted with the understanding that it should be moved there so soon as accommodations were secured."

The church was originally called "Church in Christ Jesus by the Name of Antioch."

In 1845, they moved to Fanthrop, using the lower floor of the Masonic Hall building, and, at the same time, shortened the name of the church to simply "Antioch at Fanthrop."

In 1852, the name was changed to "Anderson Baptist Church."

In 1855, using native stone dug by slave labor, they erected their own building. This building served continuously until 1955, when it burned, leaving only the stone walls. It was rebuilt, using the same stone walls.

Although it has been through several name changes, several buildings and many pastors, the Anderson Baptist Church has functioned continuously since 1844, and continues to serve its members, and the community, today. And, we could argue that it's at least a semi-country church.

Wesley Chapel Methodist Episcopal Church

HOUSTON COUNTY

"Records probably were lost in the tornado."

Located northwest of Crockett, just off FM 229, the Wesley Chapel Methodist Episcopal Church was formally organized in 1903, on land donated by J. C. Wooters. There already was a cemetery there, at the time, dating back at least as far as 1885 (there are some graves there that are still undated and unidentified).

Very little information exists regarding the early days of the church. We know that the original trustees were J. W. Craiger, A. W.

Wesley Chapel Methodist Episcopal Church

Vince, T. J. Simmons, W. N. Brown, William Burton, E. J. Curry, David Webb, and J. T. Murray.

In those early years, there was also a school building located there—actually the school pre-dated the church, and remains of the old brick and concrete cistern still stand.

We know that a Rev. Hodge was pastor of the church in the late 1920s and early 1930s. Other than that, we have no records of the history of the church. It appears the church and cemetery probably functioned as one in those early years. Due to a declining population in the area, regular worship services ceased in the early 1940s. In 1953, a tornado destroyed the church. It is likely that the church records were lost in this storm.

The church building was rebuilt, using as much of the original wood as they could find, and continues to serve as a gathering place for the Wesley Chapel Cemetery Association.

Mrs. Vera Rosson Dishongh served as secretary of the Cemetery Association for twenty-two years, and, as she puts it, "I have very close personal ties to the cemetery—and the church. My grandfather, Joe Rawls, lived next to the second school building (built about 1913). It was destroyed and he was killed in that tornado in 1953."

"We have an annual homecoming event the second Sunday in June. Lots of folks who have ties to both the cemetery and the church "come back home" for this event."

He Heard That Call!

"And he responded to it . . . in a hurry."

Sometime in the 1940s, at the church were I grew up (the Evans Chapel Methodist Church) we had a preacher that was somewhat unusual. Brother Smith (that's what we'll call him) was a good preacher and a good man . . . but he was somewhat . . . "vertically challenged." He was barely five feet tall . . . and he was somewhat sensitive about it. On the other hand, his wife, Sister Smith, was an unusually tall lady. She was about a head and a half taller than he was.

Now, Sister Smith was a good, Christian woman, but she wasn't overly blessed with patience . . . and . . . she could be a little bit domineering, at times. Okay . . . she was a whole lot domineering . . . and Brother Smith was scared to death of her.

Sometimes Sister Smith would even interrupt Rev. Smith in the middle of his sermon to publicly correct his grammar or correct what she perceived as any other mistakes he might have made.

After the end of our 11:00 o'clock service, it was customary to stand around and visit for awhile before leaving. Occasionally, however, Sister Smith would become impatient and would get tired of waiting for Brother Smith to finish his visiting. She would simply go outside, get in their car and start honking the horn. She would continue honking until he got there.

Now, this was one "call" that Brother Smith never failed to heed. In my mind, I can still see Brother Smith heading for the door of the church, just as fast as his short little legs could take him, trying not to break into a trot . . . all the while desperately trying to look as if he had simply been ready to leave, anyway.

Plaiŋ Baptist Çhurch

HOUSTON COUNTY

"We're just plain folks."

"I've been Secretary of the Plain Church since 1936" says Mrs. Bertha (Green) Best. "I was just a teen-ager then, and I guess nobody else wanted the job, so they just gave it to me, and I've had the job ever since, except for between times when the church was without a regular pastor for a short time. Some of those that served temporarily were Ray Jones, Shirley Bennett, Annie Conner, Bessie Lou McKinney and Carol Metz. Some of the clerks that served before me were A. R. Montgomery, Ollie Minton, and Addie Mae Conner."

Located northeast of Ratcliff, on CR 1170, in the Plain

Plain Baptist Church

223

Community, the church is believed to have been organized around 1880 and was originally located across the road from the present site, on the Drennan property. It is said the community got its name from the plain people who lived there—they described themselves as "just plain folks."

Some of the early families in the community were the Conner, McKinney, Drennan, Dowdy, Sibert, Wells, Sides, Duren and Best families.

Around 1916, the church was moved across the road to its present site. The building burned sometime after that—it is not known for sure in what year. In 1923, the present church building was erected. The City of Ratcliff gave them an old Woodmen of the World building and the men of the church tore it down, hauled the lumber to the present site, and built a new church.

Some of the early pastors were Rev. Higgenbotham, Rev. Pyle, Rev. J. L. Kee, Rev. Finis Schoklier, Rev. Doyle McCilney, and Rev. Scott Tatum. (In 1999, Rev. and Mrs. Tatum returned to the Plain Church to celebrate their sixtieth wedding anniversary).

"The Plain Church has been like family to us" says Mrs. Best. "It was a big influence on us when we were growing up. It helped shape our lives. It was always the social center of the community, as

Mr. and Mrs. J. A. Best, celebrating their sixtieth wedding anniversary at the Plan Baptist Church.
—Courtesy of Mrs. Best

well. My husband and I celebrated both our fiftieth and sixtieth wedding anniversaries there at the church. There just wasn't any other place we would have wanted to go to have our celebration."

"Our membership is down now . . . so many of us are old and sickly. We usually have about ten to twenty folks at our services. We still have services every Sunday—Brother Buddy Jones is our pastor. We're going to hang on as long as we can . . . we just can't give it up . . . the church is so very, very important to us."

Mt. Calm Pine Top Baptist Church

LEON COUNTY

"We're not sure about the name, but we know Rev. Norris was our pastor for fifty-five years."

In 1908, a group of settlers in the Pine Top Community, southeast of Centerville, decided they needed a church. One member of the group, Phil Johnson, donated the use of an old house—and they were in business. According to information in "The History of Leon County," the first pastor was Rev. B. G. Woodars. Apparently, they continued to worship in temporary quarters until 1917, when they acquired the property still being used today.

The church went through several pastors in those early

Rev. Jeff Norris, from funeral notice
—Courtesy of Laura McLeod

years . . . Rev. Woodars, Rev. C. H. E. Reed, Rev. T. A. Turner . . . until 1916 . . . and then they didn't have another pastoral change for 55 years. In 1916, the church called Rev. Jefferson Norris, a prominent and well-known preacher in that portion of Leon County, and he remained as pastor until his death in 1971, at the age of ninety-six. As was a common practice in those days, Rev. Norris was pastoring at least one—and sometimes two or three—other churches at the same time.

One of the first problems Rev. Norris tackled was providing for a permanent facility for the church.

He succeeded. According to Leon County Deed Records, on November 17, 1917, Phil Johnson, et al, deeded a three acre site to the Trustees of the Mt. Carmel Baptist Church (Vol. 209, Page 457). The deed is very clear . . . it was the Mt. Carmel Baptist Church . . . yet today it is known as the Mt. Calm Baptist Church. Mrs. Dorothy Johnson, a lifelong member of the church, explains the confusion this way, "All my life, it was called Mt. Calm. What I always heard was that way back then, the folks sort of slurred the word when they pronounced it, and over the years, it got shortened to Mt. Calm. After awhile, they just accepted it as Mt. Calm."

It is referred to as Mt. Calm Pine Top to differentiate it from another church, in Centerville, also bearing the Mt. Calm name.

Mrs. Johnson remembers Rev. Norris well. "Rev. Norris baptized me when I was a young girl. He lived in the Evans Chapel Community, between Leona and Flynn. That was about fifteen miles away, and he had to travel by wagon at that time. He couldn't make the round trip in one day. What he would do was come over here on Saturday afternoon, and spend the night with Frank and Lula Taylor. Then he would preach on Sunday and go back home on Sunday afternoon. It was a tough schedule, but he was used to it."

Mt. Calm Pine Top Baptist Church.

By all accounts, the present building was erected in 1917, or shortly thereafter (soon after they acquired the property) under the leadership of Rev. Norris. It is apparently the only permanent facility the church has ever had. There are many, many folks living today in Houston, Dallas, and other areas, that can trace their roots—and their heritage—to this tiny little church.

The Mt. Calm Pine Top Baptist Church still functions today, although the membership is small. The present pastor is Rev. Raymond Freeman. The little building still sits there, in its somewhat secluded location, nestled in a grove of pine trees, on FM 1119, just as it has all these years. The building has been somewhat modernized on the inside, but it still looks much the same as it must have looked when Rev. Norris was traveling by wagon to preach there so many years ago.

Stubblefield Baptist Church

HOUSTON COUNTY

"Drunkeness, profain swearing, dancing and gambling is prohibited by this church."

Although the early history of the Stubblefield Baptist Church, located about six miles southwest of Kennard on CR 4690, is somewhat vague, it is believed the church was formed as a "split-off" from the Old Ivie Baptist Church. The reasons for that division have long since been lost. The church derives its name from the Stubblefield Community in which it is located. The community, in turn, is named for W. M. Stubblefield, who settled there after the Civil War.

Mrs. Lillian Gibson has done extensive research on the history

Mrs. Lillian Gibson
—Courtesy of Mrs. Gibson

of the Stubblefield Church, and according to her research, existing minutes indicate the church was organized in 1872 and was located near the Stubblefield School. In fact, for a while at least, services were held in the school building. Mrs. W. M. Campbell was church clerk, and members included L. A. Ainsworth, Cornelina Ainsworth, James Helton, T. D. Suttles, Ann Suttles, W. L. Gates, and Sarah Gates. Rev. T. D. Suttles signed the minutes and officially approved the organization of the church, with Rev. W. L. Gates as the first pastor. The church was originally called the

New Ivie Missionary Baptist Church. It was many years later—in the 1930's—that the name became simply "Stubblefield Church."

The first two buildings erected by the church burned. The third one—the one still there—was built in 1926.

Although records are sporadic, there are minutes showing that in 1925, the church revised its "Rules of Decorum" as follows: Rule XIII—"Drunkeness, profain swearing, dancing and gambling is prohibited by this church" . . . Rule XV—"Money shall not be the judge of fellowship in this church." These minutes also state that "The (name is deleted) had trouble with drinking and worse. They went over to United Pentacost following. Heresy was the word used by the church secretary."

Records also show that Cole James, a nephew of the infamous Jesse James, was a member, but was "dropped for intoxication." Mrs. Gibson recalls hearing stories of another member, in those early years, who, after having too much to drink, rode his horse into the building during the middle of a Saturday night church service. Apparently he was removed, along with his horse, without any resulting damage or injury.

The 1926 minutes showed a membership of 122. They withdrew fellowship from four members that year. The pastor's salary that year was $90. Few records exist prior to 1925.

During the depression years, Mr. and Mrs. Edd Lenderman gave

Stubblefield Baptist Church.

the church 11.5 acres of land so the membership could grow cotton on it to raise money to pay the preacher.

The church discontinued regular services during the 1950s, due to a declining population. The building and grounds are still maintained and kept up—in spite of a problem with deer hunters sometimes trying to use the building for a camp house—this is the reason for the "No Camping" sign on the building. The church is about to receive its "Historical Site" designation and plans to mount the official plaque where the "No Camping" sign presently is placed.

Once a year, there is a "homecoming" program held at the church—when descendents of the old families come back home to visit and reminisce. Local citizens make all the preparations for this event.

As has been said by a number of folks in the area, "If that old building could talk, it could tell lots of stories."

More Churches

St. Luke's Baptist Church, Waller County

Chapel Baptist Church, Madison County

Bethana Baptist Church, Leon County

Gospel Lighthouse Church of God, Houston County

New Prosperity Baptist, Wharton County

Boone's Bend Church of God, Wharton County

Friendship Baptist Church, Leon County

West Mt. Olive Baptist Church, Ft. Bend County

About the Author

TERRY KEELING was born June 9, 1938, in Leon County, Texas. He grew up there in the Leona-Evans Chapel community on a farm/ranch, along with his parents, Roddy and Ruby (House) Keeling, and a younger brother, Royce.

In 1956 he graduated from Centerville High School and in 1960 he graduated from Sam Houston State University in Huntsville with B.S. and M.Ed. degrees.

The next few years he was engaged in the cattle and feed business in Leon County. In 1967-1969 he taught school and coached. In 1969 he moved to Houston and entered the real estate business. For the next 36 years he continued in this profession, selling farms and ranches, the last 25 of those years in Richmond.

In 2005 Terry moved to his farm in Leon County and semi-retired to devote more time to his two passions—writing and photography.

He began writing in 1999 with a book titled *Tales of Jackasses, Bee-hunters and Coffins (and other Assorted Redneck Things)*. Since that time he has had numerous short stories published in various magazines. Most of his writing carries a great deal of humor and nostalgia.

As his next project he plans to publish a book composed of a collection of his short stories.